EMBROIDERY
Ideas
LACKWORK

44

EMBROIDERY
Ideas
FROM BLACKWORK

PAT LANGFORD

Kangaroo Press

Acknowledgments

My thanks to:

My family who are always there for me.

Toni Valentine for those many hours and wonderful photographs.

Jackie McDonald, who kindly did the typing.

All the friends and workshop participants who have let me use their work: Margaret Wilkins, Patricia Reynolds, Glenys Gudgeon, Karma Bains, Helen Whelan, Effie Mitrofanis, Yvonne Wilcox, Cynthia Sparks, Muriel King and Judy Barnett.

My editor Anne Savage for her help and understanding.

EMBROIDERY IDEAS IN BLACKWORK

First published in Australia in 1999 by Kangaroo Press
an imprint of Simon & Schuster Australia
20 Barcoo Street, East Roseville NSW 2069

A Viacom Company
Sydney New York London Toronto Tokyo Singapore

© Pat Langford 1999

National Library of Australia
Cataloguing-in-Publication data

Langford, Pat.
Embroidery ideas from blackwork.

Includes index.
ISBN 0 86417 861 1.

1. Blackwork embroidery. I. Title.

746.44

Set in Palatino 10/13
Printed in Hong Kong
Produced by Phoenix Offset

10 9 8 7 6 5 4 3 2 1

Contents

Introduction

I have always enjoyed the counted thread and pattern-making of blackwork. I find the building of geometric patterns very pleasing, as there is just no end to the possibilities. I also enjoy playing with tone—contrasting thick and fine threads, large and small patterns and stitches.

There is such a mix of techniques being used at the moment, with an interplay of one technique against another. This book looks at how blackwork fits into this current trend, and how such things as painted fabric, crayons, added fabrics, layered fabrics, cords and ribbons add to the richness of blackwork. Techniques such as beading, wrapping and pulled work also add to the contrast of counted thread patterns. It is very hard to keep techniques in their own compartments. It is because of the possibilities of this grand mixture that I started off in so many directions . . .

There is much discussion as to when and where blackwork started. There has long been a popular belief it came from Spain and so it was referred to as Spanish blackwork. Historically, however, it is often impossible to pinpoint the precise source of a technique. Counted thread patterns on evenweave fabrics seem to have been a natural development in embroidery around the world, with many countries in Eastern Europe supporting peasant industries for centuries.

Blackwork was used widely on garments from approximately 1450 into the early seventeenth century. Few examples remain from this period; as the designs were a popular form of patterning on clothing and household linen (made from white linen or cambric), constant use and washing meant most pieces were thrown away when they became worn. The iron (ferrous sulphate) used to dye the black silk thread soon turned an unattractive blackish brown. There are some examples to be seen in museums such as the Museum of Costume in Bath and the Victoria & Albert Museum in London.

Portraits and miniatures are the richest source of examples of blackwork. Costumes of the Renaissance were rich with fur, padding, jewellery and embroidery. Portraits such as those by Holbein illustrate an extravagant period of decoration, where embroidery of every kind was used, from goldwork to quilting, with bands of blackwork in exquisite patterns on the collars and cuffs of white shirts.

Stippling or seeding with fine stitches fill shapes outlined with backstitch lines; patterns outlined in black silk are worked inside the lines with a mixed thread made by wrapping two strands of silk, one black, one white, around each other. These techniques seem to imitate contemporary book illustrations. The patterns were stitched directly onto an evenweave fabric, as the embroiderers of four hundred years ago did not have squared paper to work out their designs.

The late Middle Ages saw a vogue for embroidering underlinen. The shirt was worn by both sexes of the wealthier classes. The feminine version was called a smock (Anglo-Saxon) or chemise (Norman). Generally made of linen, but sometimes of silk, they were decorated at the neck and wrists with gold or coloured silk. At the close of Edward IV's reign 'slashing' (slitting) the outer garment came into fashion, with the shirt being pulled through the slits to show further decoration.

Through the time of Henry VIII and into the Elizabethan period, blackwork moved from decoration on dress and clothing accessories onto a variety of household articles. Linen continued to be used into the sixteenth century by those who could afford it, in such household articles as sheets, towels and napery, as well as wall hangings. The arrival from Spain of Catherine of Aragon as Henry's first wife encouraged the fashion for this style amongst the upper classes. A Moorish influence can be seen in the geometric patterns which appeared at this time: stars, circles, interlacing, quatrefoils, lozenges, rectangles and arabesques.

Male dress became more elaborate and exaggerated. Many different layers of garments became the fashion,

Man's nightcap. Linen, embroidered with black silk and silver-gilt thread in stem, long and short, herringbone and plaited braid stitches. English; late sixteenth century. Victoria & Albert Museum, London

worn open in front and showing each layer. The shirt now became elegant attire, made of extremely fine fabric, even sometimes transparent. Sumptuary laws passed in both Henry's and Elizabeth's reigns dictated what should be worn by various ranks of society, forbidding extravagant dress to the lower orders.

In 1553 an Act of Parliament was passed forbidding everyone below the rank of knight to wear 'pinched' (pleated) shirts or 'plain shirtes garnished with silk gold or silver'. The reigning monarch set the style. One of the King's *Inventories of Apparel* contains entries of 'shirts wrought with black silke'.

A New Year's gift for a nobleman of the period was 'smocks wrought with black silk Spanish Fashion'. As seen in portraits of the time, Spanish work was delicate in its beginning but developed in richness as clothing became more lavish. It is first shown on the neckbands

and wrist-bands of shirts and chemises, then on standing and turndown collars, the fronts, wrists and sleeve frills of men's shirts and on the shirt sleeves pulled through slashed sleeves. In portraits of women blackwork is seen on wristbands and chemise fronts, and on a separate garment called a partlet. This was a covering for the shoulders and the upper part of the chest which was buttoned down the front, at first collarless but with a standup collar added from about 1530. The male version was usually called a plackard. Lord Monteagle's *Inventory* in 1523 listed 'Eight partlets, three garnished with gold, the rest with Spanish work'.

An important factor in the progress of embroidery in the sixteenth century was the appearance of pattern books. Just one copy exists today of a book printed in England in the year 1548 featuring arabesque designs.

Detail of long cover. Linen, embroidered with black silk in braid, chain, coral, back and buttonhole stitches. English; second half of the sixteenth century. From the Lord Faulkland Collection, Victoria & Albert Museum, London

The early seventeenth century saw the demise of blackwork as embroiderers looked in other directions, but by the late nineteenth century the climate had changed again. 'History', in many forms, became popular, and Victorian embroiderers supported numerous exhibitions of historical embroidery, including Elizabethan domestic embroidery. This interest led to the twentieth century revival of blackwork, a selective revival in which embroiderers concentrated on a few elements. It seems the filling patterns were of particular interest, developing into a recognisable style emphasising the patterns. As happened with so many other techniques, however, the vigour of the original embroidery was overlooked by these early twentieth century embroiderers. They put many techniques almost into a 'straightjacket', claiming a 'right way' of executing them. Through the influence of books and stitch magazines this kind of attitude spread rapidly. In the case of blackwork, double running stitch as an outline stitch was favoured, overlooking traditional stitches such as chain, satin, back, coral, braid and detached

Woman's bodice. Linen, embroidered with black silk in stem, back and running stitches with speckling. English; late sixteenth century. From the Lord Faulkland Collection, Victoria & Albert Museum, London

buttonhole. Mrs Christie continued this 'right way', emphasising Holbein stitch and pattern filling in hard-edged shapes.

By the 1960s new life was injected into blackwork through the Needlework Development Scheme of Great Britain, which had a beneficial influence on all kinds of embroidery during this time.

Blackwork continues to be very popular with embroiderers. The pattern-making is so satisfying, the idea that you can just get yourself some squared paper and draw up your own patterns. Just to take a piece of evenweave fabric and start stitching is so pleasing. (Of course people have always had a strong urge to put the world into some sort of order, and pattern-making has this sense of order!) But there is more to it than this—the greatest satisfaction comes from building the tones in a design, changing tonal value just by changing the thread or by opening the stitch, making it larger or more

spacious in its interpretation; the many threads that can be used, the many textures of one colour, thick, thin, soft, coarse . . . wool, cotton, silk, linen or rayons.

One of the most important things, of course, is to use an evenweave fabric, one where you can see the threads easily. Try different counts of fabric; some people enjoy working with fine fabrics, others with something a little coarser. I do use the fine weaves but I enjoy the more open weaves because of the effects I can achieve with the heavier threads. Do try different threads and materials to discover some of the many possibilities. The other important twentieth century change, is of course, the introduction of colour . . .

Later in the book there is a graphed section showing some of the dozens of filling stitches that can be used. I'm sure that you'll come up with many variations of your own. None of them is named, as they are just that—filling stitches.

Twentieth century works

A small selection of works from twentieth century embroiderers showing some of the directions in which blackwork is being taken.

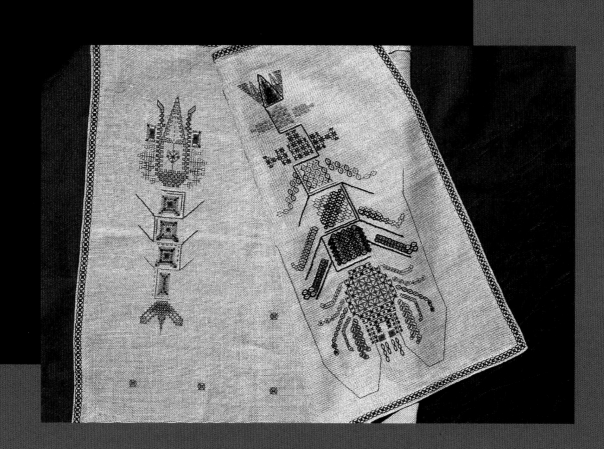

Crayfish table topper

CYNTHIA SPARKS

This table topper by Cynthia Sparks is an example of the style of the mid-sixties. A mixture of line and space filling with irregular edges and not remaining tightly within a rectangle. This is very much in the style of the period. A very successful use of stitches with a good balance of tone, achieved by variety in weight of thread.

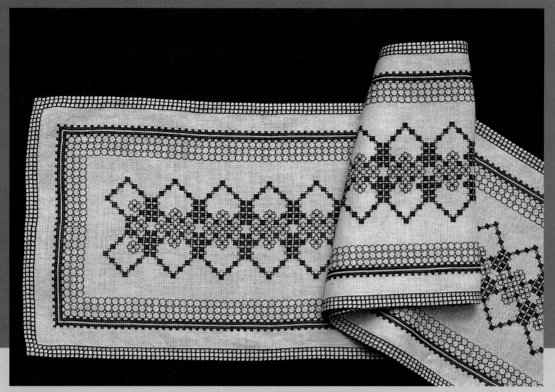

Table cloth and runner YVONNE WILCOX

This octagonal table cloth and matching runner are both worked in a traditional manner on Lugarno fabric. The table topper is stitched with DMC Perle 12 and Kreinik Metallics Balger cord. Double running stitch or Holbein stitch was used for the centre design and filling stitches. The chain stitch inner borders are whipped with Balger cord. The Picot edge stitch is three Hedebo buttonhole stitches worked over three threads. Four-sided stitch is worked between the picot and the whipped chain outer border.

Tasselled cushion EFFIE MITROFANIS

Effie's cushion was inspired by a historical design on a man's coif using a repeating scroll pattern. Effie's interest in repeating patterns and geometric grids is part of her wider investigation into different grids and their possibilities in many fields of embroidery.

Elizabethan mind's eye
EFFIE MITROFANIS

Effie wanted to combine a head with a geometric grid and thought this Elizabethan head with its heart-shaped face and rounded hair ideal; the shape was extended to a point to create a tear-drop motif which was repeated in a half-dropped pattern, repeating patterns being a theme of blackwork. Effie used stem stitch with gold twist and passing thread on padding, with painted paper and pen and ink drawing.

Bird landing
MARGARET WILKINS

This embroidery was based on a newspaper photograph. The darker tone on the far wing is important, giving a sense of movement. The subtle colour change in the background gives a suggestion of grass on a hillside behind the bird.

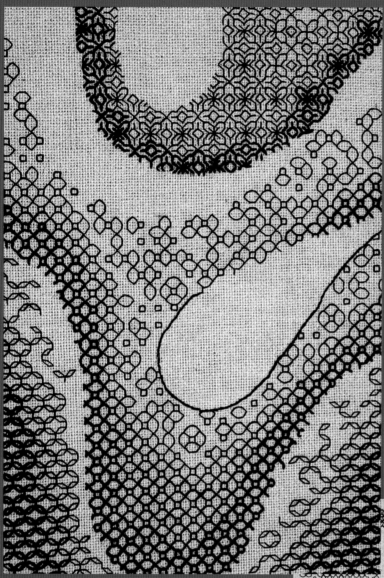

The wave

MARGARET WILKINS

This work started from an aerial photograph of Sydney Harbour, but there are many changes from the original picture. Many of the lines in the original changed to the wave movement which has become the dominant element. Every stitch now seems to add to the dominant rhythmic flow of line with constantly changing tonal patterns.

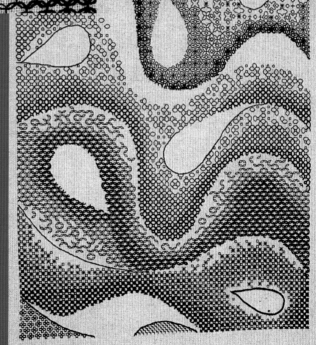

Sunday afternoon pattern: coffee at the Opera House

A black and white photograph of people sitting under the awnings on the forecourt of the Sydney Opera House was the starting point for this piece. When I took this photo I was intrigued by the strong tonal contrast of the sunlit area and the dark shadows cast across the people.

The patterns followed the photograph closely to simulate the positive and negative arrangement of the tones. I used a fine Lugarno fabric, DMC Perle 8, coton à broder and one strand of stranded cotton in a variety of blues and greens. Small patterns suggested the fine grain of the photograph.

The design was transferred using tracing paper: a careful tracing of the photograph was pinned to the fabric, I worked small stitches along the lines of the design, then I tore away the paper ready for stitching. I used a green velveteen fabric for the mount.

The details show the fine stitch interpretation—both blackwork and pattern darning.

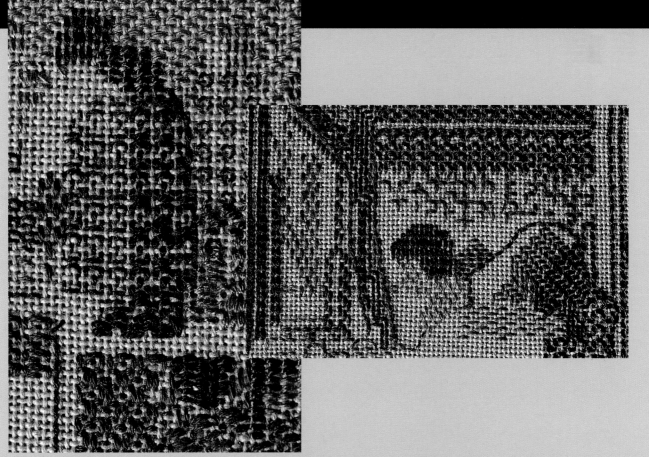

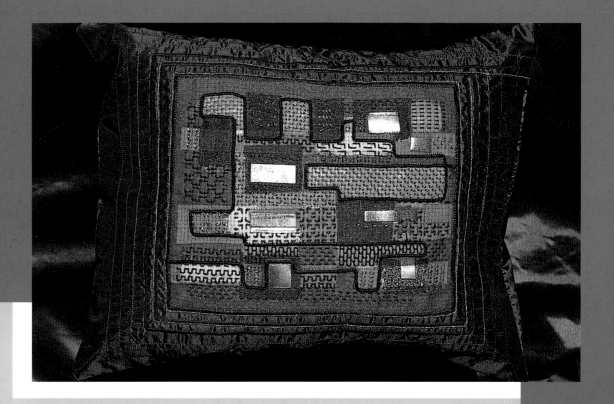

I used a background of white Binca cloth for this cushion panel, with a small quantity of gold paint stroked onto it. I laid a layer of blue organza across the Binca cloth with small square pieces of extra organza and rectangles of gold kid sandwiched between the fabrics. I machined a continuous line of gold around and over the rectangles to hold the pieces in place, then added a continuous line of black couching to emphasise the more important rectangles. Areas of the organza were then cut away to add to the contrast of tone and texture. Simple darning patterns added surface interest beside the more elaborate blackwork patterns. I machined the decorative panel onto the sympathetic blue silk background fabric, adding self-coloured lines of couching interplayed with machined lines of gold.

Blackwork & layering

The next group of embroideries mix blackwork with layering, a technique I developed for a workshop. This is a very useful way of building the tonal pattern which is very much part of the character of blackwork. The machined couching is such a direct way of establishing the design, but is something that can always be done by hand if the embroiderer prefers.

Although using the same basic technique, each of these works has developed in very different ways. It is always interesting how students interpret a technique. The piece by Muriel King on page 30 has a very rich variety of stitch, with embroidery over all the box top.

The work baskets use pulled work in metal thread to add richness of contrast to the surface.

Autumn I

A simple arrangement of shapes and stitches, using shapes cut from organza. Darker tones were made by placing extra organza shapes underneath the covering layer of organza; the lighter tones were created by cutting pieces away from the covering layer. A mixture of machine-stitching and hand-stitched blackwork patterns complete the textural effect.

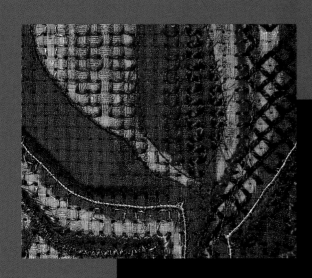

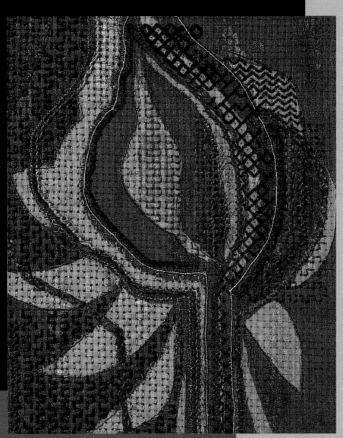

Autumn II

'Autumn II' is worked on Binca canvas. I used dry brushwork, keeping just a little paint on the brush and dragging it across the fabric, just letting the paint soak into the hollows. Pale blue, gold and Indian red were the colours used. I then laid a layer of organza over the fabric and machined around the large leaf shapes, adding thick threads which were machine couched to outline the main shapes of the design. The leaf shapes were then cut away to reveal the background fabric.

Simple blackwork stitches were then added in broken areas, just covering the fabric freely with irregular edges rather than filling a shape completely. When completed the work was dry pressed on the reverse side ready for stretching onto a board for framing.

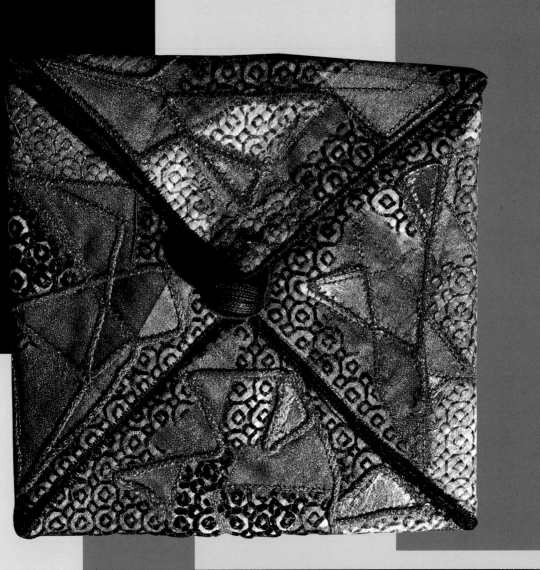

Gold evening bag

This envelope bag begins with a very simple 20 cm (8") square of white Binca cloth. My first design element was gold paint, applied freely in triangular shapes. Then I cut randomly sized small triangular pieces of gold kid and organza and pinned them in place on the Binca cloth underneath a transparent gold fabric.

Continuing the triangle as the design element, I machine couched a continuous line onto the fabric. This could have been done by hand in back stitch. A gold line was added by the same method. I then cut away shapes from the transparent gold fabric to reveal different tones of gold ready for stitching.

The one blackwork pattern stitch is carried right across the fabric using different weights of thread to add to the tonal pattern. The thicker thread is DMC Perle 8 and the finer threads are one, two or four strands of Marlett, a shiny thread, as contrast. I also worked the stitch in gold, using DMC Fil argent clair. The bag is lined with a brown silk and iron-on Vilene. A thick thread was machined around the edge to make a strong finish. The corners were folded to the centre and stitched by hand, with a fat bead and buttonholed loop added as a fastener.

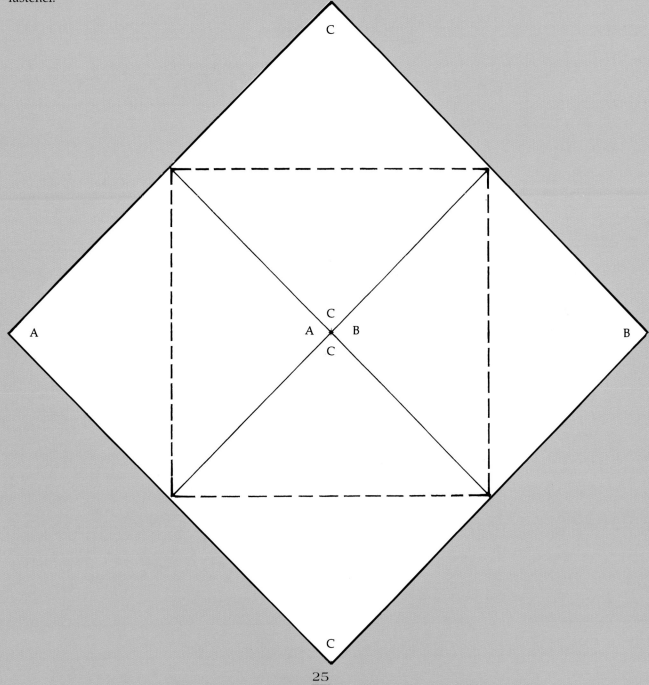

Blue
evening bag

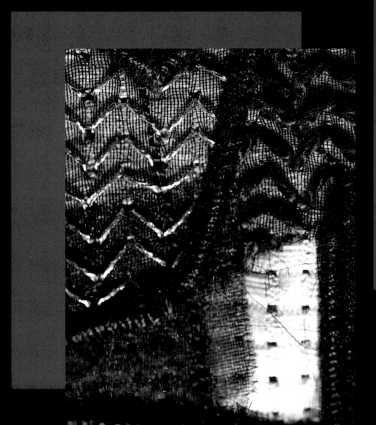

The finished bag is 30 cm x 20 cm (12" x 8"), just large enough to hold a small purse and a few necessities for an evening out. Blue gloving leather, gold kid and silver kid are the starting points for this design, worked on white Binca cloth with an overlay of blue organza. A line of machine stitching, starting in the centre of the piece and working out to the edges, fixes the basically rectangular design shapes. It is important to always start the stitching in the centre and work out, as this will prevent any puckering of the organza, whether you are stitching by hand or machine. I machined a heavy thread around most of the shapes.

When cutting the organza away I deliberately did not cut too near the edge to avoid fraying the thin fabric. I allowed about 2.5 cm (1") to wrap over the edge of the Binca fabric for a good finish.

The stitching was worked in DMC Perle 3 and 5, navy blue; a grey shiny thread and DMC Fil argent clair (silver) and a fine aluminium thread.

Making up

I used a navy blue linen mix fabric to line the bag with an iron-on Vilene interlining. To get a blue line around the edge of the bag I allowed 1 cm ($^3/_8$") extra of the blue fabric all round. The edge of the stitching already had the organza wrapped over it, giving a good edge as it sits on the navy. I then stitched a line of navy thread 5 mm ($^3/_{16}$") in from the edge to firm it, then couched a thread in navy blue all around the edge.

The piece was made up into a bag by machining just inside the couched line.

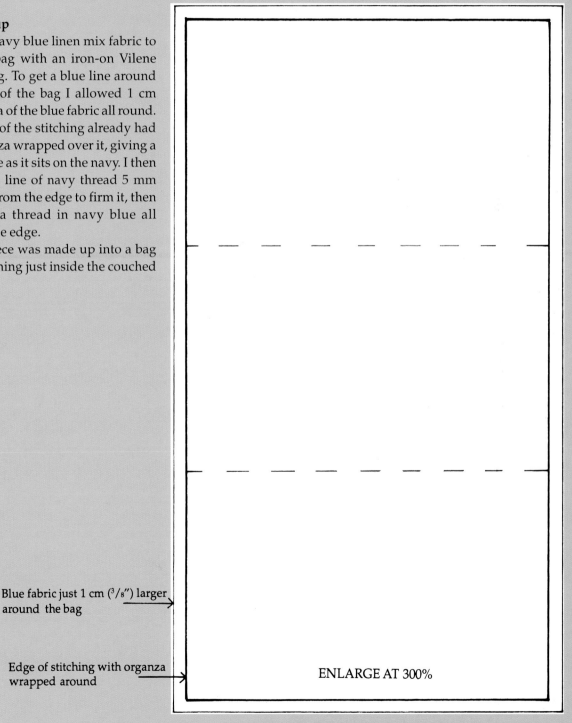

Blue fabric just 1 cm ($^3/_8$") larger around the bag

Edge of stitching with organza wrapped around

ENLARGE AT 300%

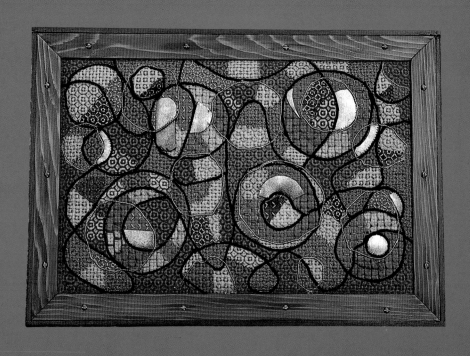

Wooden box top
MURIEL KING

This box top by Muriel King is a rich arrangement of patterns using the layered technique, with a layer of organza over the fine Binca fabric. A free line of thick black thread was trailed over the fabric and couched down; some of the embroiderers in this group machined the thread down, but others used hand couching. A gold thread was also couched onto the fabric, in random rounded shapes. The organza was cut away in places showing the background fabric, and small pieces of gold kid were fitted into some of the shapes. Many different filling patterns in gold, white and black thread produced an incredibly rich final effect.

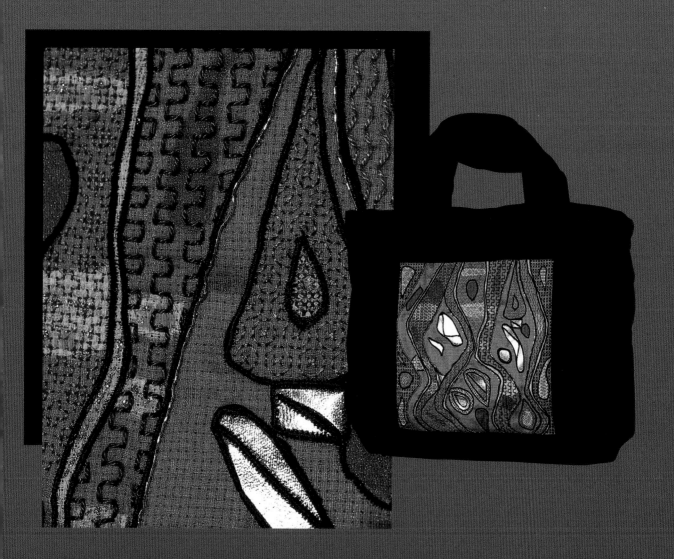

Blue bag

JUDY BARNETT

This complex panel was created in the same class as the box top by Muriel King on the opposite page.

Judy used a blue, gold and black colour scheme, starting with random spots of gold paint and patches of silver kid and blue organza on white Binca cloth. A gold thread and a thick black thread making vigorous rhythmic shapes were couched over an organza overlay which was later cut away in places to reveal the fabrics beneath. Filling patterns in black, gold and blue thread contribute to the richness of the overall effect.

Houses in the dark
PATRICIA REYNOLDS

This work illustrates Patricia's interest in the patterns formed by houses, and the many different roof shapes to be seen in group housing. Different arrangements of windows, the textures of walls against plain areas, are all interpreted in strong tonal balance using layers of fabric added and cut away, lines of couching and simple filling patterns stitched in black, white, grey and gold threads.

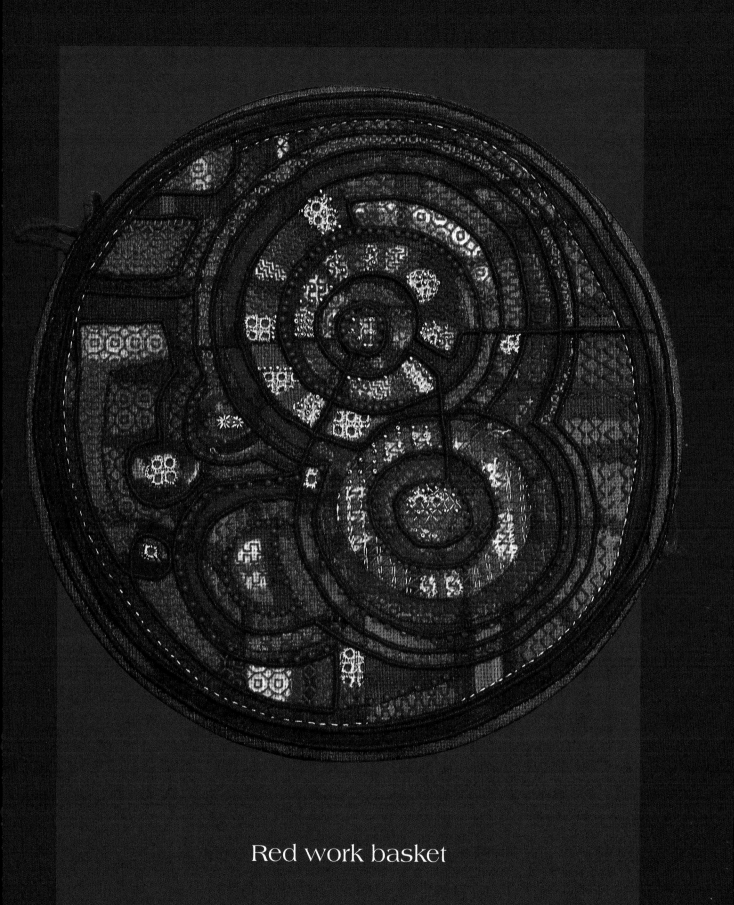

Red work basket

This is an interesting way to cover the top of a work basket. You need to know the exact size of the top of your basket before you start, so turn it upside down on a sheet of paper and trace around it to get an accurate measurement.

This design was worked on a loose weave white fabric, beginning with thin acrylic paint in reds, pinks and gold applied in free-flowing circular shapes, a simple arrangement of circles overlapping to make many smaller shapes. If you would rather draw the design on paper first, using a compass and ruler, make the lines very dark so that you can see them through the fabric to trace the design with brush and paint. Keep the paint thin so that it does not clog the spaces of the fabric.

I laid a layer of red organza over the base fabric, followed by a layer of black organza, pinned the three layers together and assembled them in an embroidery frame. I used a circular frame 30 cm (12") in diameter. I machined a thick dark red thread around all the lines of the design.

The next step was to cut some of the black organza away to reveal the red. I find this is a very exciting part of the embroidery, just slowly cutting the layers away, sometimes cutting both layers to show some of the background. It is the many variations of shapes and subtle colour changes that emerge which are such fun.

The patterning was worked in various tones of red, from bright orange to very dark brown-red, using DMC Perle 8 and fine Marlett. One circle was filled with orange and gold, in the other I used rectangles of gold eyelets and gold beads.

The red and gold beads add to the contrast of texture, plus the metal threads used for the pulled work add another effect to the surface

I cut two pieces of board ready for mounting. I used heavy boxboard, sometimes called strawboard.

When the embroidery was finished I pressed the stitchery on the back and laid a piece of a glitzy red fabric under the embroidery to show through the pulled eyelets. Then a piece of pelham was laid over the board between the board and the work. (Measure the work 2.5 cm (1") larger than the board, machine on the line before cutting.) A row of tacking was worked approximately 1 cm (³/₈") in from the edge.

Place the embroidery on the board, putting pins into the edge of the cardboard in order to keep the work in position.

Turn the embroidery over and pull the tacking thread tight to hold the work in place ready for lacing.

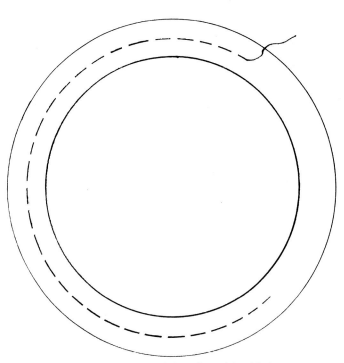

Large tacking stitch around the edge of the fabric

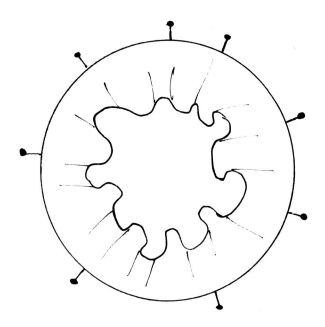

Underside of lid with tacking thread pulled tight ready for lacing

To line the lid

Cut a piece of card just 2 mm ($^1/_{16}$") smaller in diameter than the boxboard. This time I used mountboard which is not so heavy. Cut a piece of fabric 2.5 cm (1") larger all round than the card. I used a fine woollen fabric, a layer of pelham for interlining, and calico.

Prepare in the same way as the embroidered top, with a row of tacking pulled tight ready for lacing.

Place the two pieces back to back and slip stitch together.

The basket is lined at the base. There are many different ways of lining baskets but for this one just a soft lining seemed sufficient—a piece of light card covered with calico, pelham and lining fabric resting in the base of the basket. The basket seemed rather stark in colour so I stained it with thin red acrylic paint.

The needlecase and scissorcase both use the same elements of design as the top. The two 12 cm (5") circles of board making the outside of the needlecase are lined in the same way as the basket top, using slightly smaller circles of board for the lining. Use lighter board to suit the needlecase's small size. Two bars of buttonhole stitch make the hinge. A bead and buttonholed ring form the fastening.

The scissor case is made the same way as the small blue scissor case on page 111, from a 20 cm (8") square of embroidery, using the method described there.

Blue work basket

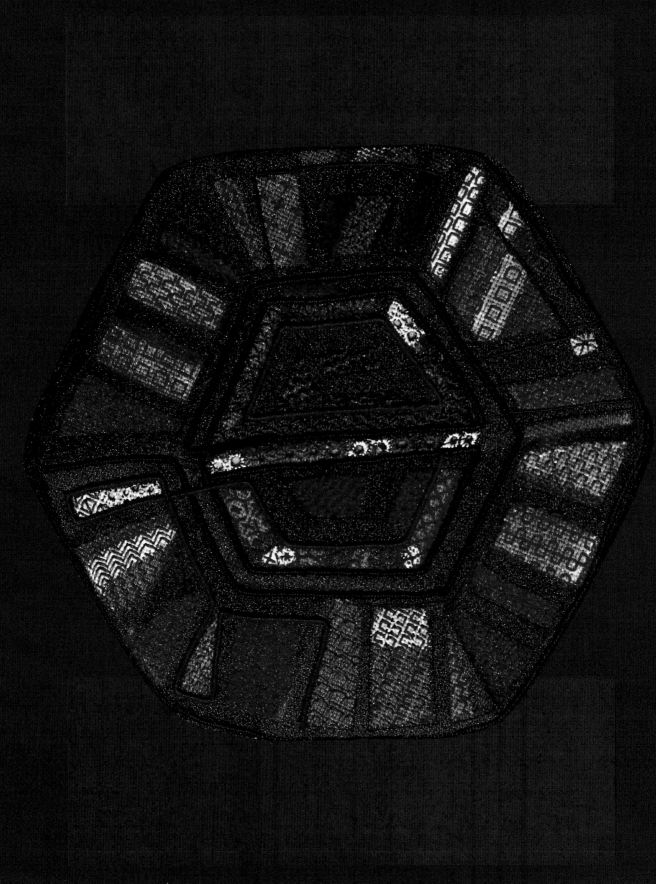

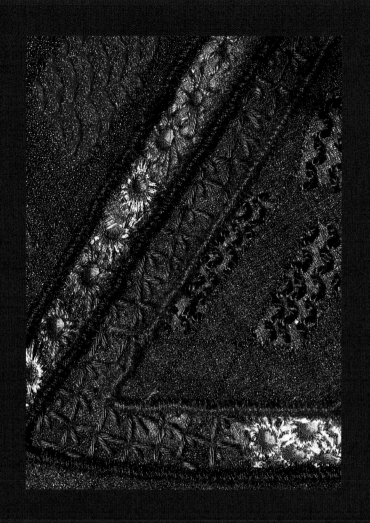

The design on this basket lid follows the hexagonal shape of the basket. The six sides of the basket being slightly irregular, it was important to be accurate with the pattern outline, matching the angles precisely. The embroidery was worked following the same technique used for the red work basket top, using blue acrylic paint as well as red and gold, and a blue organza overlay.

Basket tops using beads

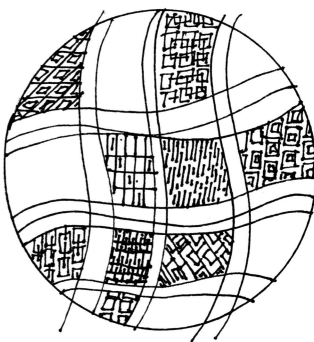

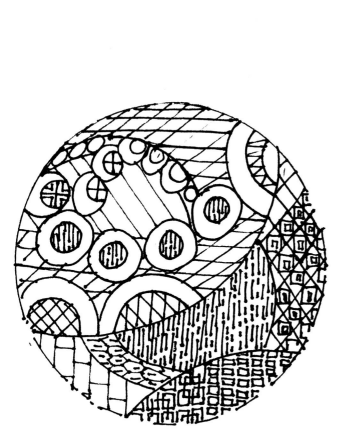

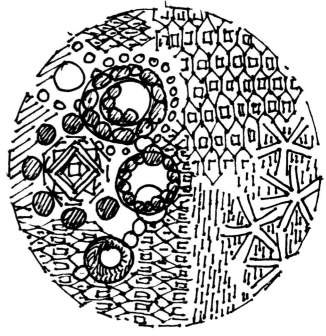

Beading to establish the designs
before filling with stitches

Other techniques

Daisy bag

This is an idea for a highly decorative bag which it seemed to me could be thought of as a bag of celebration. Each side of the bag is built up with a collection of individual daisy shapes, four flowers on each side.

Photocopy the drawing at 150%, then trace the flowers from this pattern, continuing the hidden parts.

As most evenweave fabrics come in a range of colours, each flower could be worked on a different coloured background, or you could paint the background fabric instead. Set the fabric up in an embroidery frame and work each flower twice, one for each side of the bag; if your frame is large enough, you could do both at the same time. Use a variety of stitches and textures on each piece to give each flower a different character.

The completed flowerheads are backed with same colour fabric, either bonded together or laid together and machined. You could lay a thread of tapestry wool, or perhaps the thickest thread you have used in the filling stitches, around the edge under a row of satin stitch. Trim the fabric close to the satin stitch, then add another row of satin stitch around the edge for a strong finish.

Making up

The bag is very simple in construction. Cut four rectangular pieces of fabric following the sizes given on the pattern diagram, and allowing for turnings, and two pieces of pelham without turnings.

Lay two pieces right sides together with the pelham on top. Machine the pieces together, leaving the top open. Trim the curved edge ready for turning. Turn right side out and press. Make the other side the same. Turn the top edges in and slip stitch. Machine a firm wide satin stitch around the edge of both pieces. Add a line of satin stitch 3.5 cm (1¼") down from the top edge.

To join the sides machine a fine straight stitch just beside the satin stitch, from point A to point B as shown on the diagram.

Finish by adding a handle of one or several lengths of interesting hand-made or machine-made cords, fixed just behind points A and B.

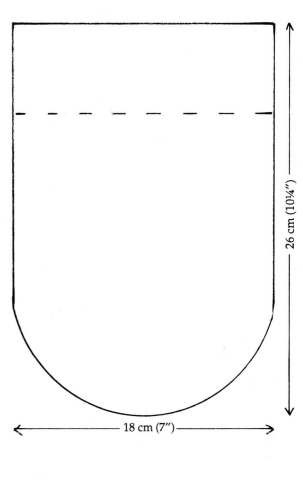

26 cm (10¼")

18 cm (7")

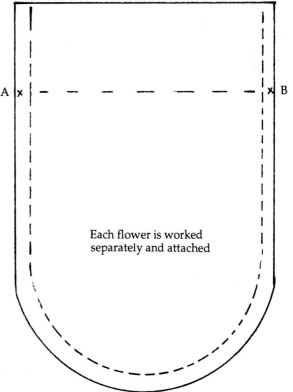

A x   x B

Each flower is worked separately and attached

Blue box

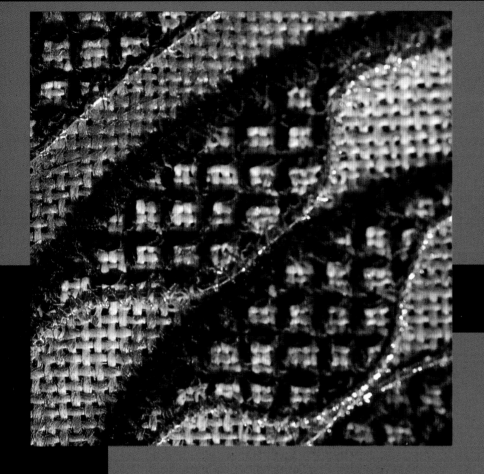

This work box illustrates a very simple design arrangement. The blackwork panels were embroidered first on white evenweave cloth, then machine-sewn to navy blue linen-mix fabric ready to be made up into a box. The embroidered panel on the top of the box is approximately 16 cm (6¼") square; the side panels are approximately 16 cm x 8 cm (6¼" x 3¹/₈").

I started by painting roughly circular shapes on the fabric for the top of the box in mid-blue and gold paint. On the four sides the circular theme squashed down to an oval.

Simple wavy lines of thick navy blue and gold threads set the shapes to be filled in with a square filling pattern in navy blue. The very centre features a different filling stitch.

Each of the four sides is slightly different, as I allowed the wavy lines between the ovals of heavy stitching to evolve quite freely. Each side was worked using the square pattern as a linking stitch, again with a different pattern in the centre.

The finished pieces of embroidery were machined onto the navy blue fabric and outlined with navy blue and gold machined lines.

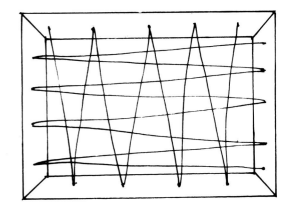

Making up
Cut two pieces of card for the top and the base (boxboard is the most suitable) each 19 cm (7½") square. Cut out four pieces for the sides each 19 cm x 12 cm (7½" x 5") for the sides. Sandpaper the edges.

Cut the embroidered fabric panels to fit the pieces of the box, allowing 2 cm (¾") turning all round to lace the panels over the card. Back each embroidered panel with calico cut to the same size.

Stretch each embroidered panel over their respective pieces of card and lace tightly with linen thread.

Line the inner side of each piece of the box with the same navy blue fabric, again backed with calico. Stitch tightly to the outer layer, covering the lacing and making sure the lining will not be visible from outside the box. Cover both sides of the box base the same way.

Machine the edges of a strip of fabric approximately 18.5 cm (7¼") long and 2 cm (¾") wide—just fold, machine and turn out—and slip stitch between the back and the lid to form a hinge. Pin the box sides to each other and to the base at the corners and slip stitch into position with strong navy blue thread.

Machine the edges of a strip of fabric about 12 cm x 2 cm (5" x ¾") and slip stitch the ends inside the lining of the top and one side of the box to prevent the lid opening too widely.

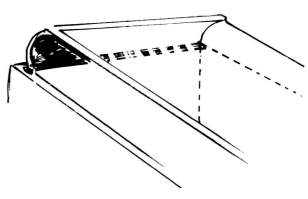

Fabric used as main hinge

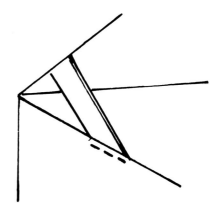

Hinge slipped into the side of the box, the other end slipped into the top

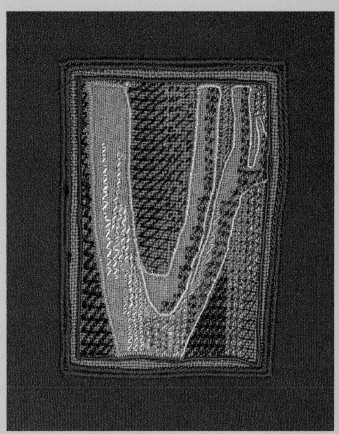

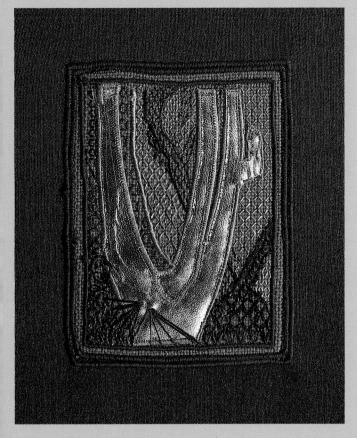

Three trees

On deep gold backgrounds these three exercises treat the same basic tree shape in very different ways. In the first embroidery the greater part of the stitches were worked in the same direction across the work to suggest a shaft of light through the trees. The outline of the trees was machined with a narrow satin stitch.

In the second piece I used a piece of gold kid for the silhouette of the tree, machining it down first. The outlines of two trees behind are just suggested with a fine line of machine couching. The filling patterns were then worked with a variety of threads, including DMC Perle 8 and one strand of stranded cotton.

In the third piece I used a fine gold thread for the tree outline, working a simple stitch over two threads. This uses a variety of threads in the one stitch to develop the background.

Clock tower

ROBYN ECCLESTON

This strikingly patterned and subtly coloured work was based on a photograph of the city taken from the edge of Sydney's Hyde Park. The stitches on the buildings are particularly successful as Robyn has used different patterns to suggest the heights and textures of the buildings. Using the stitches in a vertical direction emphasises the density of the buildings against a clear sky. The self coloured background receding from the intensity of the foliage in the foreground gives this embroidery an amazing depth of perspective.

Black workbook

KARMA BAINS

This piece by Karma Bains started with a drawing. Putting the grid down on paper first and then interpreting the drawing onto calico instead of using a counted thread fabric is a very different approach to that used in her other piece, 'Three Dancers', on page 48.

To complete the work Karma painted the whole surface, calico and embroidery, with black Permaset fabric paint, finally highlighting the stitching with white paint. She has used it as a cover for a hand-made book.

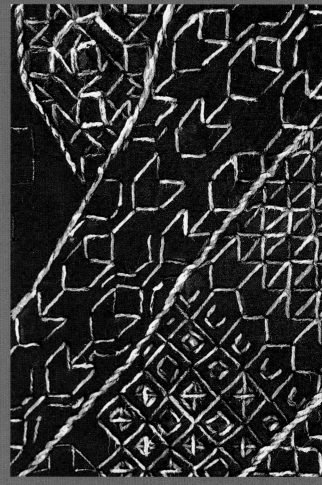

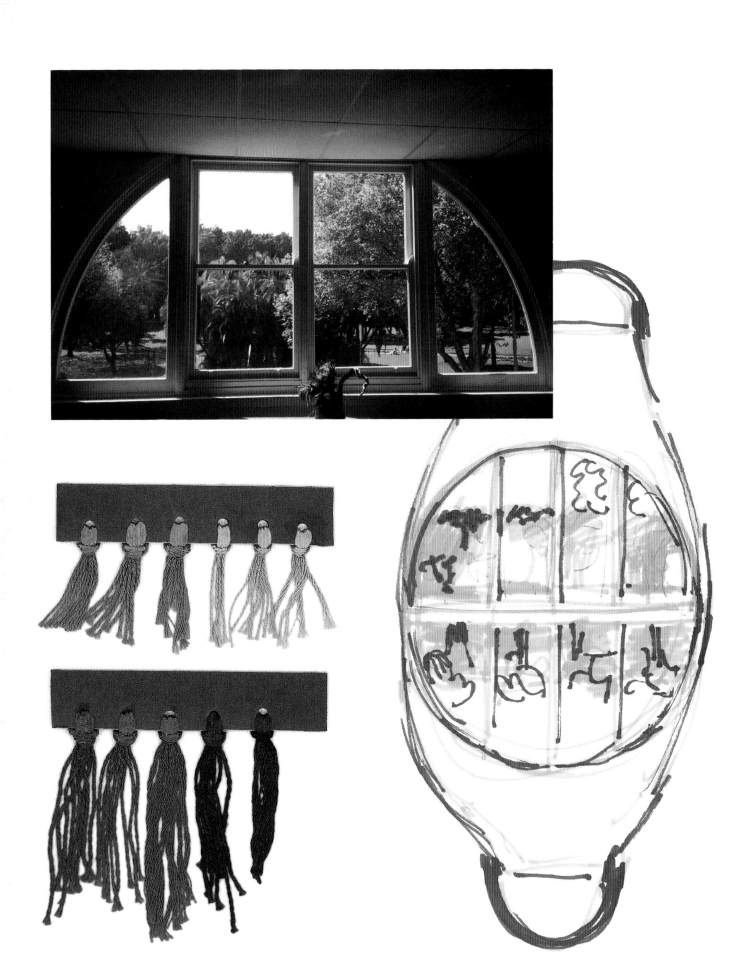

Hyde Park

The embroidery on this handbag was a fun exercise, starting with the snapshot taken through the arched window.

The vertical shapes allowed me to frame the foliage in an interesting way; the foliage itself was embroidered in a variety of filling patterns and weights of thread, worked directly onto a heavy cream Glenshee fabric in a range of dull blues.

The bag was lined with navy blue polycotton and completed with large arched handles echoing the shape of the the window frame.

The bag measures approximately 26 cm wide by 23 cm deep (10¼" x 9").

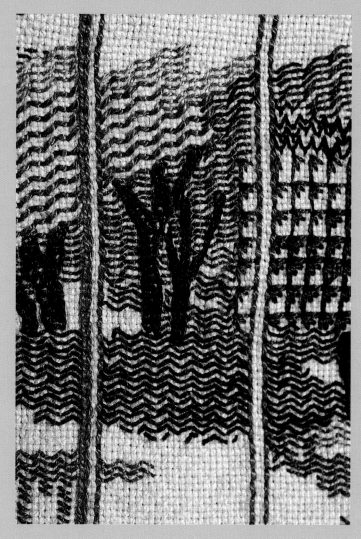

47

Three dancers

KARMA BAINS

A passion for figures and dolls was the starting point for 'Three Dancers'. From the age of twelve Karma Bains loved making wardrobes of clothes for paper dolls; this is the background to this piece of embroidery.

Karma's wonderful eye for the weights of various threads and filling stitches has brought this embroidery alive with true perspective and the illusion of movement.

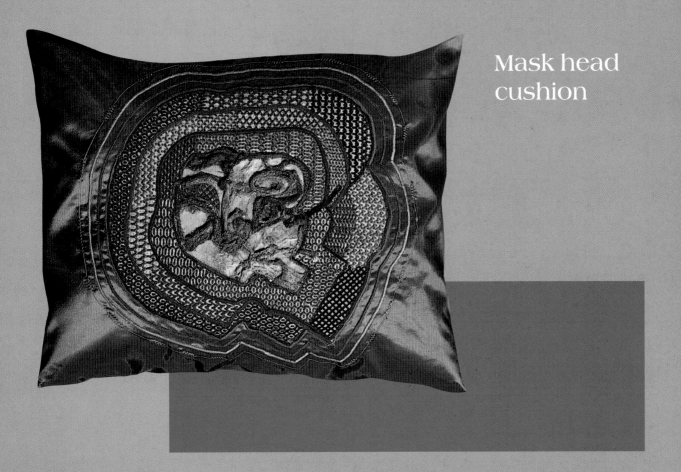

Mask head cushion

The embroidered panel on this cushion combines quite different techniques. The centre was painted on painter's canvas using acrylic paint, with heavy wools couched around the edges of the shapes. This motif was machined onto a very open Binca cloth and several lines of heavy satin stitch were machined around the shape. I used fairly heavy thread in strong colours in the filling patterns. As the Binca cloth has a very large open weave the patterns are also large and change direction as they travel around the shapes.

When the embroidery was completed it was pressed from the back into a padded surface, and a line machined around the edge. The next step was to trim the embroidery and machine it onto a polyester fabric of the same tone, ready to be made into a cushion. I emphasised the shape with a few more lines of machining.

Design sources

The reference drawings on these pages are taken from many sources, including an ancient Scandinavian tapestry and bracelet, Arabic textiles and old designs on carved ivory. Everything around us is potentially a source of design inspiration, particularly the wealth of historical reference.

Because the patterns of blackwork's filling stitches are the most important characteristic of the technique, simple geometric shapes are often suitable as the starting point of a design. Having said that, one immediately becomes aware of all the many possibilities, the many subjects one would like to interpret in the technique. I personally find all those holiday photographs are just asking to be turned into stitches.

No matter which technique they become fascinated with, it is inevitable that embroiderers will finds themselves collecting all kinds of interesting information about all sorts of things. Everything we look at, everywhere we go, interesting patterns seem to appear. It might be beach umbrellas themselves, with their patterned surfaces, or the light and dark patterns that form when they are turned this way or that to protect swimmers from the sun. Look at the patterns on those things around us, like the plates in the cupboard; the patterns and shadows they cast as they are stacked against the sink. Think about brick paving and the many ways the bricks can be arranged in different settings.

Mankind has always had the need for self-adornment; the development of this need within the many cultures of the world has produced the most glorious collection of patterns for the stitcher to use. There is an enormous range of decoration to draw from, ranging from the familiar patterns around us to the many sophisticated patterns from ritual and ceremonial around the world.

Woven tapestry, Sweden, AD1100

Gold bracelet, 6th century
Gotland

14th century Arabic textile

Baroque ivory

Barbarian art—ivory

52

People on the beach

Inside the train,
Flinders Street

Kitchen in gallery

Echuca

53

A scene from a Sunday market, with the background containing all the pattern and the figures left as silhouettes.

OPPOSITE This busy garden would need to be worked on a fine fabric, having so many small patterns and textures.

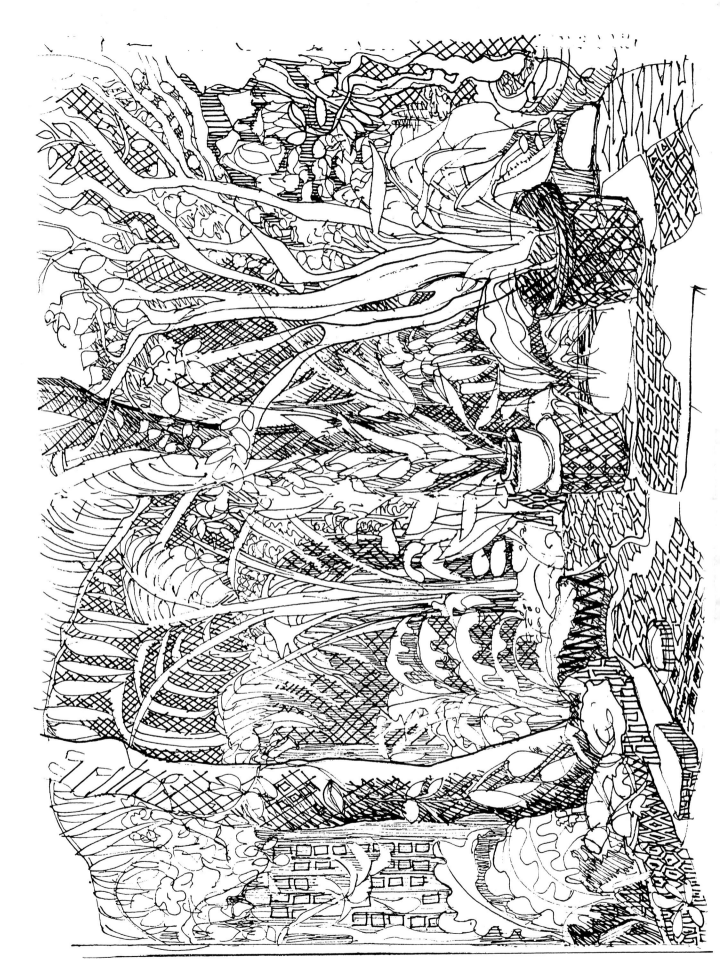

Clown heads: several interpretations of heads covered with blackwork patterns, using positive shapes filled with designs against negative shapes left empty for strong contrast.

Photo: courtesy Colin Whelan

The movement in the photograph illustrates the importance of stitch direction

Using the tonal patterns of the photograph to suggest the texture of the young animals' coats

Designs for boxes using very simple square and rectangular patterns

1. Simple curved lines flowing across the design

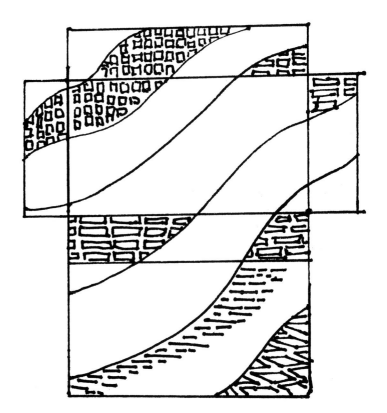

2. More concentrated patterns placed in discrete areas across the box

3. Squared divisions across the box top to hold the patterns

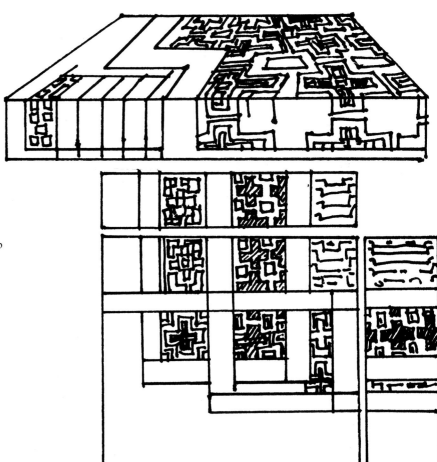

Doorways and entrances

These doorways and entrances are a collection of drawings taken either from friends' houses or from interior design magazines. Here the drawings have emphasised the contrast of the negative space against the heavily patterned surfaces.

Spanish dancers in Seville: using busy patterns to suggest the movement of the dance.

Natural patterns

Everything in nature is so beautifully patterned in structure, repetitive patterns just flow across so much of the surface in natural forms.

The seashells featured on the next two pages illustrate this point beautifully. Even within a group of shells of the same species, each shell shows variations on a theme when you look at them carefully. Groups of shells, taken either from drawings or photographs, are always the start of a good design; the shadow variations make such good tonal arrangements along with the endless variations of pattern on the surface.

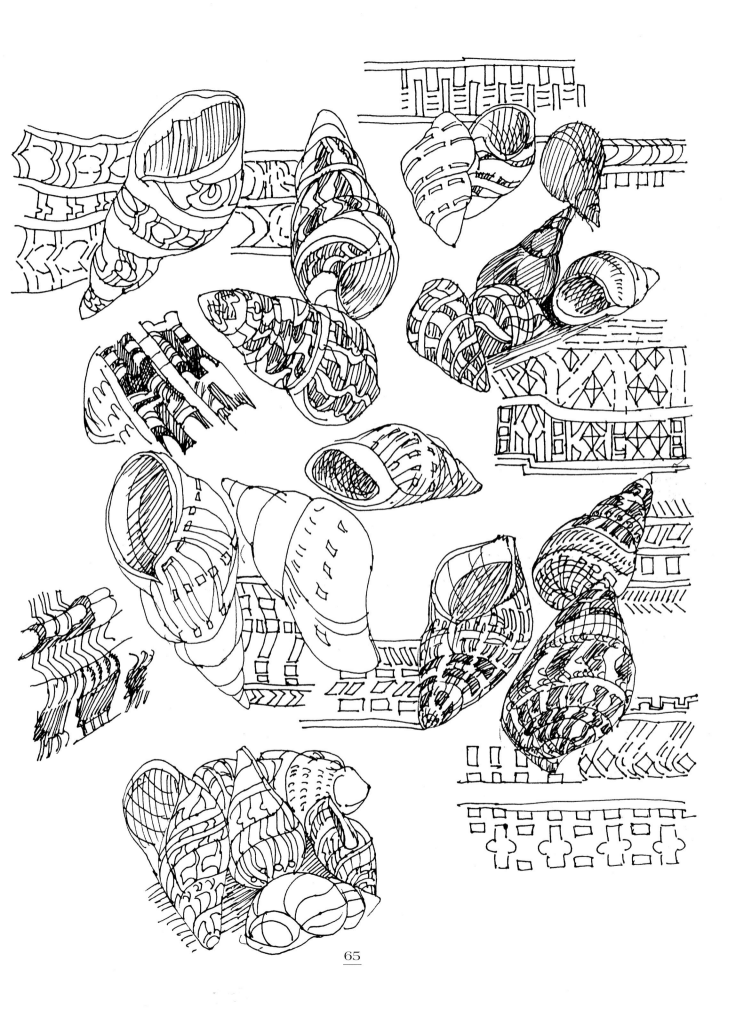

3.30 pm: Waiting for a meal

OPPOSITE This photograph of a highly patterned tree against the strong texture of the rock has many contrasts for the embroiderer to interpret in large and small blackwork stitches. Here the direction of stitch would be very important in suggesting the twist and height of the tree.

Development of a design

I often suggest using an apple as a starting point for the development of your own design, as it is something we always have around us, something we are very familiar with and used to handling, familiar with the shape and texture.

Here are a few suggestions to help direct your steps. Make as many drawings of the apple as possible—draw it from the side, from the top, from the bottom, then cut it in half and do the same again.

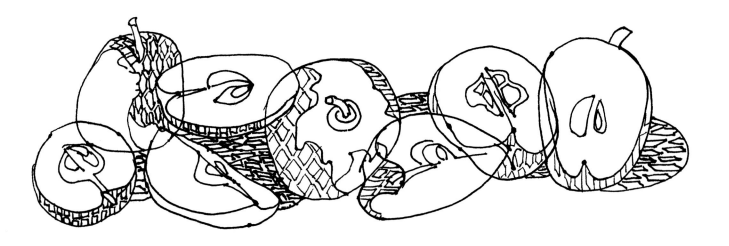

Overlap all these shapes and any others you might have thought of; arrange them into a long shape. If this were horizontal, it could suggest a border or repeat pattern.

Take the shapes again; overlap them into a circle; this could be the starting point for a design for a table cloth, perhaps a circular cloth with parts of the same design placed around the edge of the cloth.

More ideas

Look at the different places you might find an apple, and photograph it or draw it in position. The first place that comes to mind is in the fruit bowl on the table or bench, ready for someone to reach out and eat it.

Think about the apple's place in the fruit shop. It will be surrounded by many other shapes. The decorative way the fruiterer piles the fruit into pyramids, the shadows these cast; sometimes there are repeated patterns with the fruit sitting in the boxes, sometimes nestled in brightly coloured papers which add a further tone to the fruit. The square shapes of the boxes offset the roundness of the apples.

Looking back into the apple's life you might consider it still sitting on a tree, perhaps incorporating the patterns of the trees as they cross the hills of the orchard. Then you might have freshly picked apples in a decorative basket, straight from the tree to the kitchen. To take this kind of analysis even further, consider the apple in religious symbolism . . .

Stencils

The following group of designs have all been made by using stencils. Acetate, obtainable from art shops, is the material used here to produce the design. It is a very easy material to cut. A sharp cutting knife, a cutting board and away you go. These shapes were cut freehand, but if you want to use a particular design draw it on with a fine felt pen or drawing pen, allow to dry and then cut. When you are cutting a stencil it is important not to cut away too much—always leave connecting bands in the drawing. To see what the final design will be like and to avoid cutting away too much, use the pen to fill in those areas to be cut away so that you can see the final result. Leave the edge around the design to contain it (and to have something to hold onto while painting).

Iron the base fabric before you start, as creases will interfere with the final result. Work on a flat surface, either pinning the fabric to a board or using masking tape to make sure it doesn't move. Attach the stencil to the fabric with masking tape. My choice in paint is thin acrylic. Use a dry brush for painting, just wiping most of the paint from the brush. A stippling brush can be useful, as it prevents the paint creeping under the acetate.

There are endless design possibilities with one small stencil. You can repeat it, half repeat it, turn it, reverse it, repeat it in different colours. I have used fine pen lines to suggest the stitches in this group of designs.

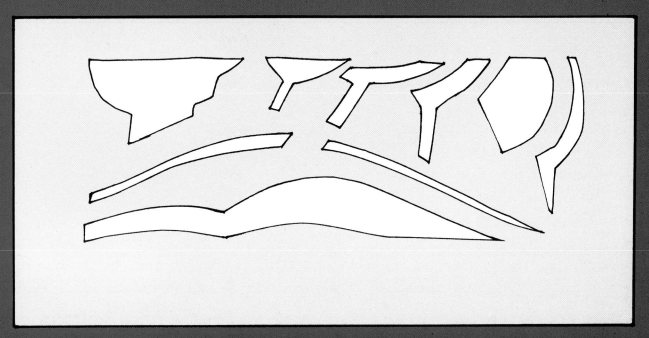

Here we have possibilities with a simple landscape.

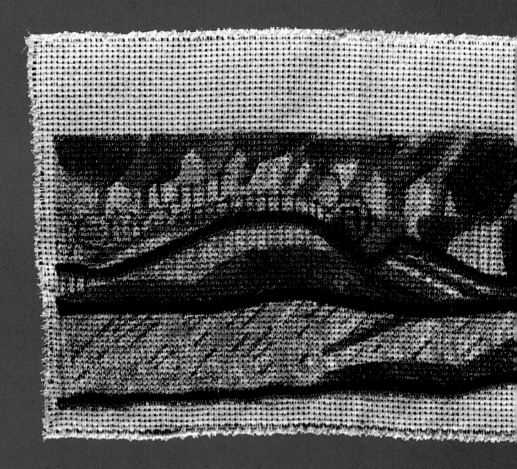

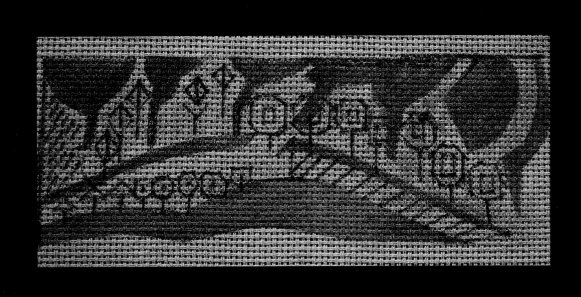

A single print from the stencil with suggested stitches

The same design printed side by side in light green with overprinting in dark green. Flicks of yellow suggest the flower heads, then I've drawn in fine lines to suggest the filling stitches.

Three prints of the one stencil were used here in different positions— yellow first, then green and blue. I've machined in some heavy lines and again suggested filling patterns with fine pen lines.

Developments from one small stencil

Designing from the materials

Each of the designs in this section evolved from the characters of
the threads and fabrics.

Jewel box

A simple pattern worked in dark brown DMC Perle 3 decorates the top and two sides of the box. The fabric is a cream Glenshee evenweave. The velvet ribbon across the top links with the ribbon on two sides of the box adding a strong emphasis to the design.

The box was made in separate pieces following the principles for the Blue Box on page 42. This box measures 18 x 15 cm (7″ x 6″), and is 5.5 cm (2¼″) deep. In this case I used a layer of thin wadding under the embroidered fabric, rather than calico, and lined each piece with a fine brown wool. The 'button' was made of a roll of ribbon, firmly stitched together, fastened with a buttonholed loop.

Circular garden

In this design suggested by a friend's formal circular garden, I started by lightly painting pale blue Binca cloth with acrylic paint in several blues, greens and yellow. On another piece of fabric I glued down random circular and oval patterns in wool and various braids, and overpainted them heavily with thick acrylic paint in the same colours. This textured piece was cut up and spread around the circle to suggest the flower beds in the garden. Filling stitch patterns between the heavily machined connecting lines in navy blue and gold are suggested by penned lines. This piece would make a very interesting top for a work box, made up following the instructions for the red work box on page 34.

Happy journey

This embroidery developed from the centre; stitching on the edge of a length of Antique braid, making it stand up on the fabric. The 'spring' of the braid seemed to find just the right spots to fall. Because this is a small piece of work I used simple stitches within the shape, offset by a plain darning stitch around the outside. Flat gunmetal grey beads emphasise the curves.

Landscape

This landscape was suggested by the paperbark which I glued to the fabric as the starting point. Some lengths of Antique cords were machined on to emphasise the shapes. Simple pattern darning worked in blocks adds the tones.

Wandering line

I started this piece with thick blobs of yellow and white acrylic paint dropped randomly onto tapestry canvas. I lowered a length of wool onto the paint while it was wet to create the framework of the design. Open blackwork stitches fill the spaces around the paint. I stitched the canvas onto a black linen fabric supported by a piece of calico, which in turn was machined to a white evenweave fabric. The open design used in the centre was then worked on the outer border. The centre stitches were worked in DMC Perle 3, 5 and 8, but I used only 8 in the outside border.

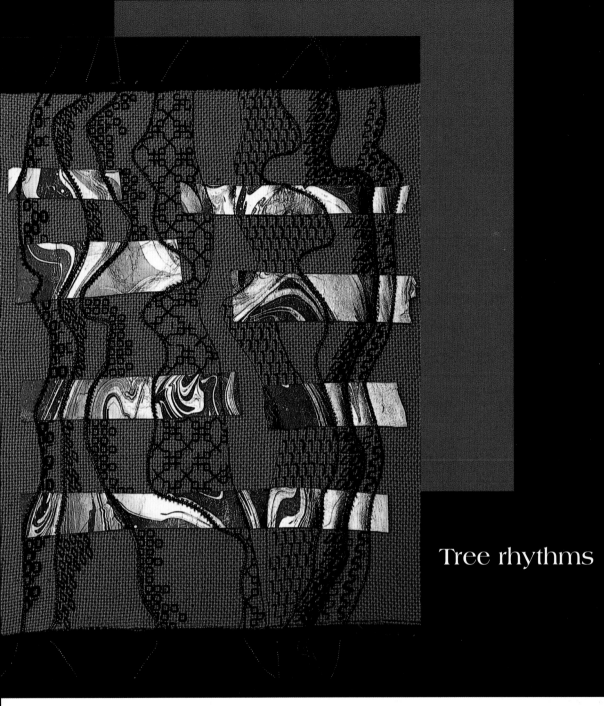

Tree rhythms

A piece of marbled kid was the starting point for this design. While doing some marbling one day I tried the colour on a piece of gold kid to see what would happen. (The rough edge of the kid can be seen on the right hand side of the design.) The free-flowing lines which appeared on the kid were suggestive of many patterns in nature, particularly the bark of some eucalypts.

I cut the kid in strips and spread them across a piece of Glenshee fabric, tacking them into place by taking the tacking threads right across the leather. I pinned some Antique braids into place and machine couched them. These lines follow the rhythms across the kid. The cut and spread method used here links the lines across the spaces between the kid. After the braids were machined in place I ran two stitched lines down the centre of the work.

The lines were the starting point for the filling stitches, kept closely stitched near the lines and allowed to thin out as they moved across toward the next line. This is a tantalising exploration as it has the possibility of being used as either a horizontal or a vertical design.

Golden pattern

Here the softness of the fabric and the draped effect contrast with the regular squares of the canvas. Using the same colours, the canvas was attached to the Aida cloth with small stitches. As the work spread across the background fabric the stitches were not completed and finer threads were used, with finally just one strand of Marlett helping the design across the fabric.

Dripping bronze

A corner of a piece of bronze kid with the natural edge of the skin making such an interesting movement. The threads used are Copper Colour 40s Twist and Antique Twist 40s. A thicker Antique thread sets the heavier parts of the design. The same threads are used to hold the kid to the background. The one filling stitch, a simple triangle, changes its format as it crosses the work and spreads across the background to soften the edge of the shape.

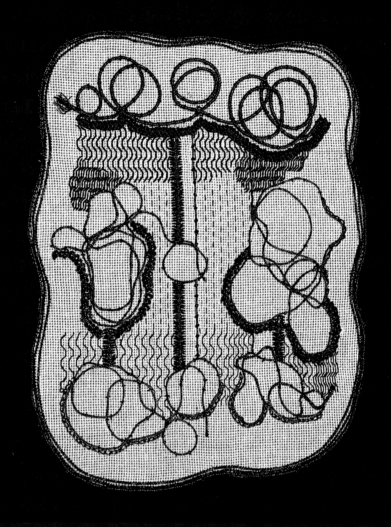

Baroque curves

Here I have really let the threads have their own way. Using Antique cords, I dropped them onto the fabric to make this Baroque pattern quite naturally. The accidental curves in the lower half of the design made very strong shapes. Because of the thick cords and strong shapes the heavier stitches such as braid stitch, rosette, chain and raised bands seemed to be just right for outlines. Simple filling stitches with a vertical accent were just right for the background to give the contrast.

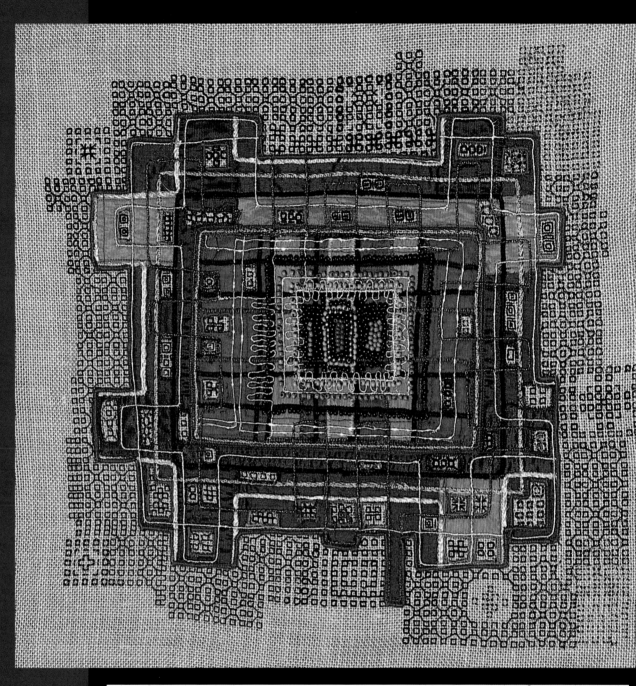

Computer board

This is an excellent example of the mix of many different techniques. The centre section of beading spread across the fabric, and machined metal threads were added to the fabric which was a collection of blue and green strips machined onto a blue background. This was then added to an evenweave fabric.

Cutting many holes through the fabrics to the lower layer reveals the blackwork patterns peeping through the spaces. The pattern spreads around the outside of the solid areas with continuing change in colour and tone and thickness, using a variety of threads such as coton à broder, Marlett, DMC perle 5 and 8, and stranded cotton. The subtle change of colour is achieved by using one strand of each colour, sometimes mixing a new colour with a strand of coton à broder and a strand of Marlett together in the needle.

Miniature bag

Wrapped balsa wood 'sweets' for a panel on a miniature bag, using shiny fabrics and blackwork background.

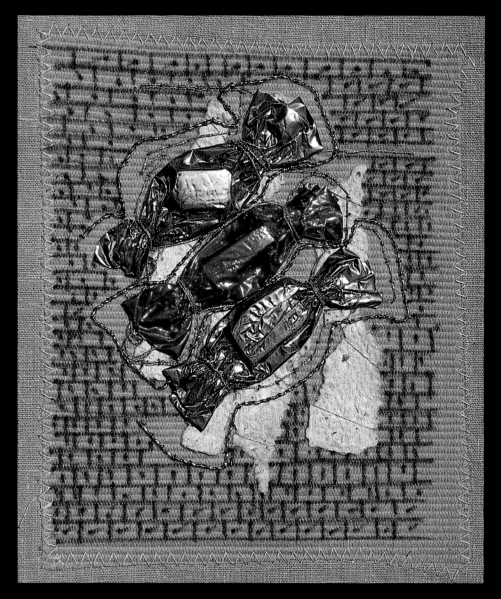

Squared tree

This piece started with the rat-tail braid, which was stitched down around the square of gold paint to define the central element. The braid is a fat round cord which sits nicely on top of the fabric. The square blackwork stitches in the centre, again in rat-tail cord, contrast with the space around the tree, and are echoed by the finer, smaller stitches in the surround. The embroidery was machined to a dark blue background fabric mount.

Suggestions from still life

There is a play of decoration here, of empty areas inside silhouettes with pattern darning giving the light tone to the background. Various size filling stitches add to the contrast of tones.

Most of the patterns here suggest contrast to the plants and fruit on the table. Note how the direction of stitch gives the flat dimension to the water in front of the vertical effect of the stitch on the back hills.

Suggestions for cushions and two book covers, using a leaf in different arrangements.

A

A Grid design suitable for a cushion or tablemat allows the four large leaf shapes to break across the centre of the article. The horizontal patterns use the same stitch in different sizes.

B

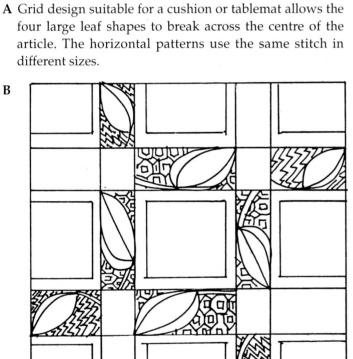

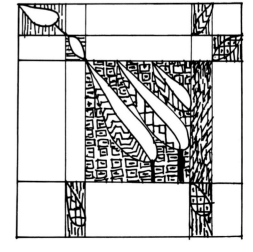

B Here squares contrast with the leaves, a different stitch suggested in each rectangle as background to the leaves.

C The panel has just four bands of stitching, with a separate rectangle in the centre as a focal point for the patterned leaves.

D The shape is again divided into smaller areas. Here vertical pattern darning is used to add another texture to the piece.

E This design contrasts with the previous one, leaving more empty spaces as rest areas against the stitched shapes.

Suggestions for handbag shapes
These different shaped handbags show ways of fitting the designs to each shape.

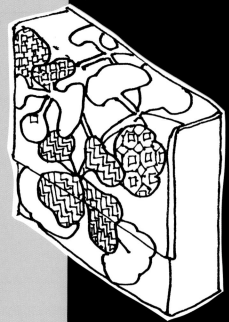

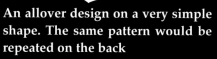

An allover design on a very simple shape. The same pattern would be repeated on the back

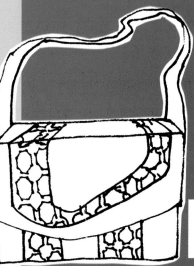

A shaped shoulder bag with a continuous panel of stitching around the bag

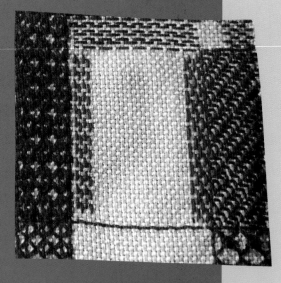

In this piece the design is broken up into separate areas across the bag

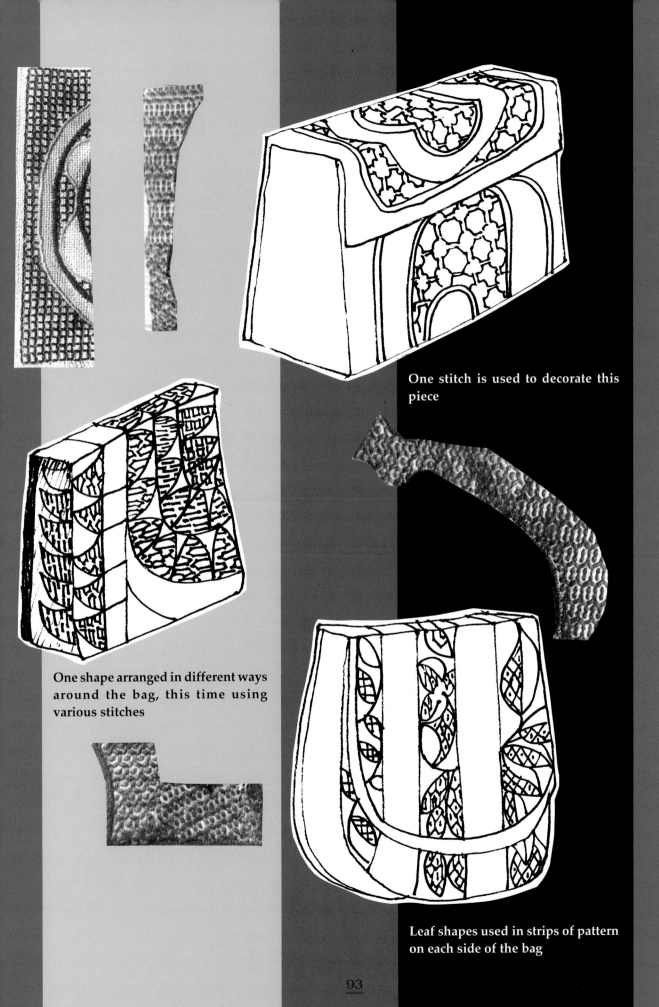

One stitch is used to decorate this piece

One shape arranged in different ways around the bag, this time using various stitches

Leaf shapes used in strips of pattern on each side of the bag

Designs taken from the hibiscus drawing incorporating a multitude of filling stitches

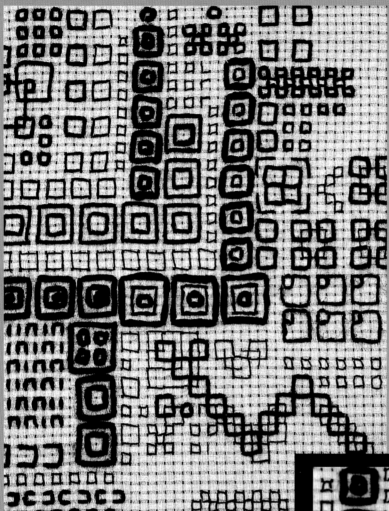

Stitch variation

In this sampler the simplest of backstitch patterns have been used in as many different ways as possible—across the fabric, overlapping, thick and thin threads, large and small.

Designing with crayon

This sample illustrates how a design can be worked up very quickly using fabric crayon applied to Binca fabric in strongly directed lines, with simple filling stitches following and emphasising some of the lines.

Sewing machine sampler

GLENYS GUDGEON

Glenys has used automatic patterns on the sewing machine as filling stitches in this attractive abstract.

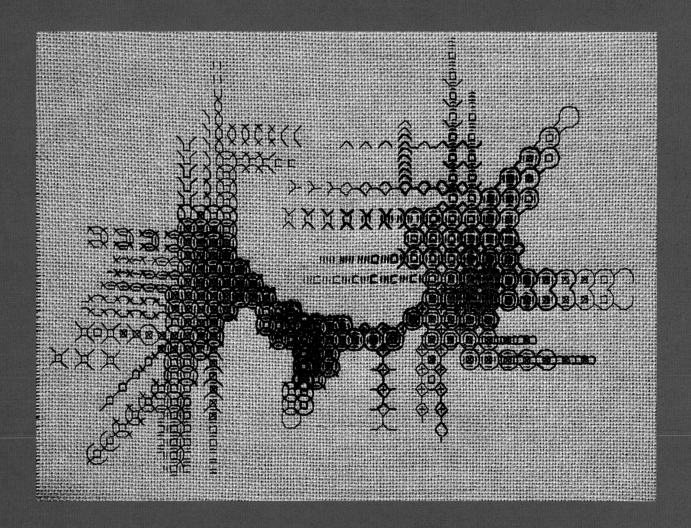

Sampler

CYNTHIA SPARKS

In this sampler the stitches flow across the work in a very free movement, the stitches changing in density as they are enclosed or spread apart, often with only part of the stitch being worked.

Cork 100 linen

Glenshee

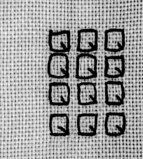

Sulta

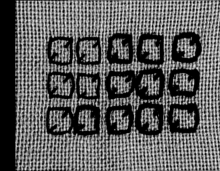

Irish linen

Cork

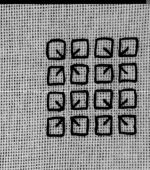

Lugarno

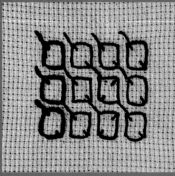

Fein Aida

Floba

These samples show different fabrics suitable for blackwork, with stitches to give just a suggestion of the possibilities for each fabric. Stitch drawings appear on pages 101–107.

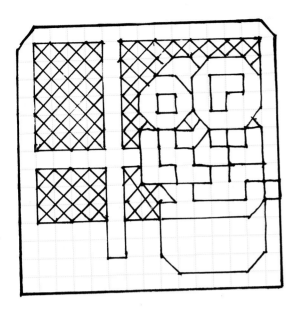

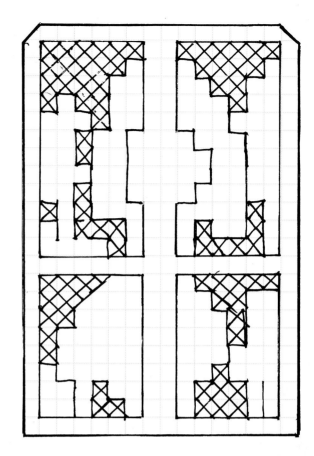

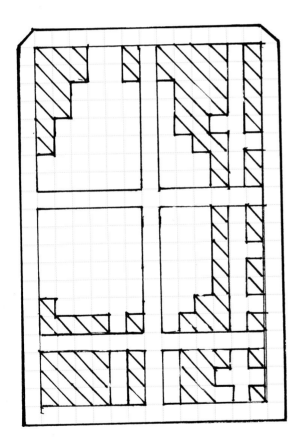

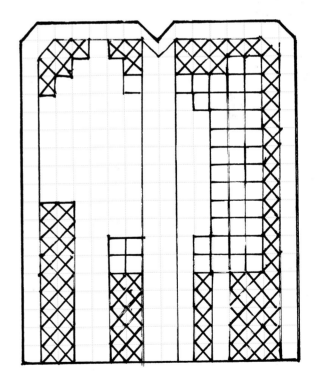

Window shapes

Designs using blackwork and window shapes, possibly as a row of 'windows' around the edge of a cloth.

Filling stitches—the heart of blackwork

These diagrams of filling stitches illustrate just how many patterns can be built around the same unit of stitch. It is great fun to just get squared paper and start making your own patterns.

None of these stitch patterns have names—they are just part of the repertoire.

The other stitches used in this book are probably commonly used by every embroiderer—couching, eyelet, satin stitch, buttonhole, chain . . .

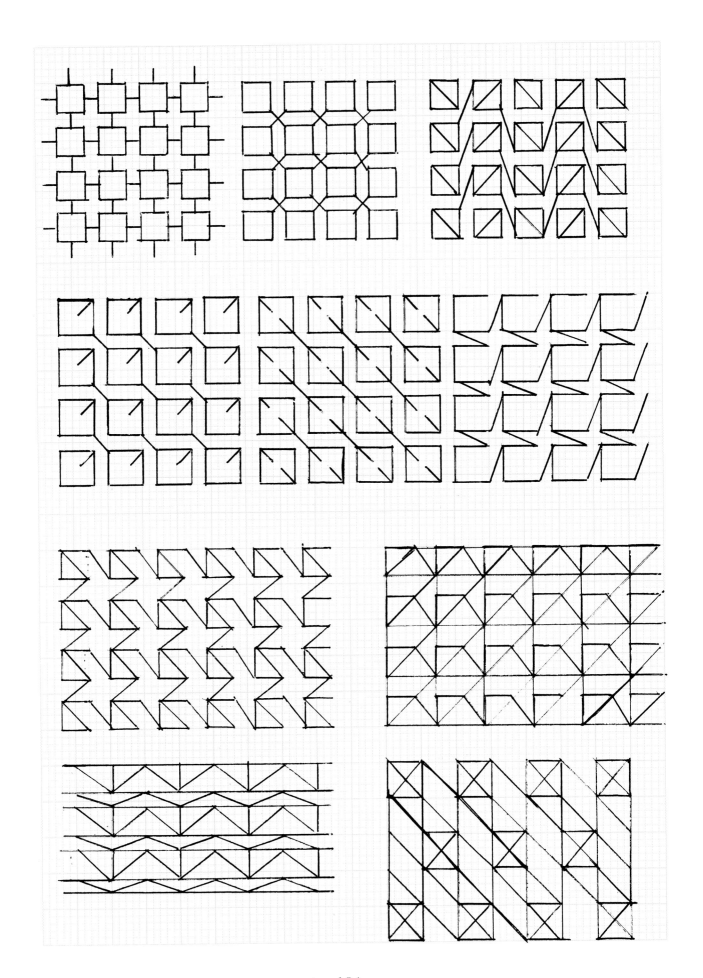

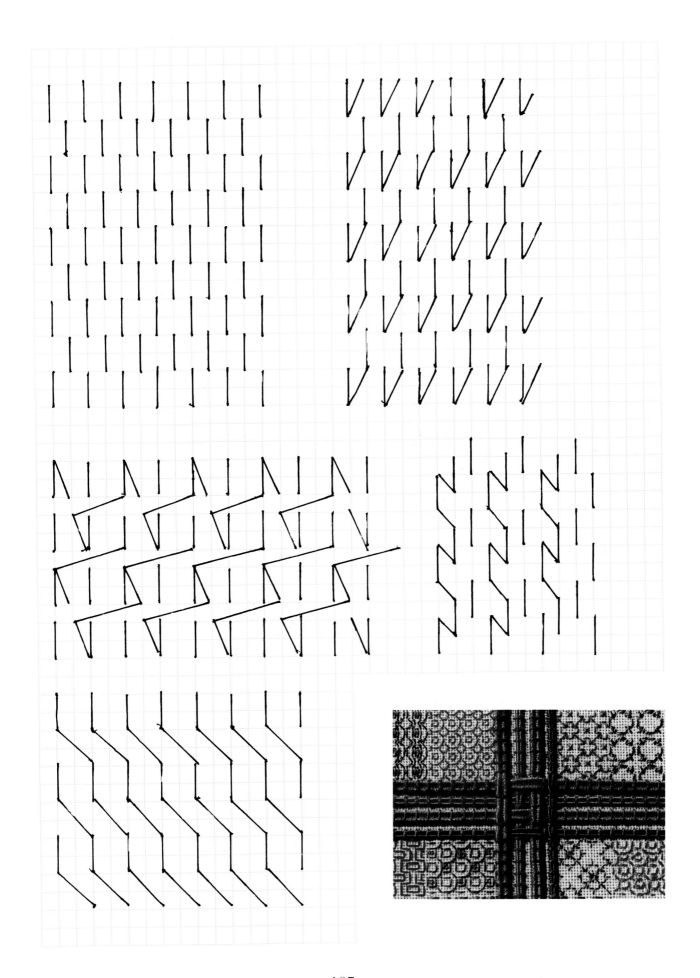

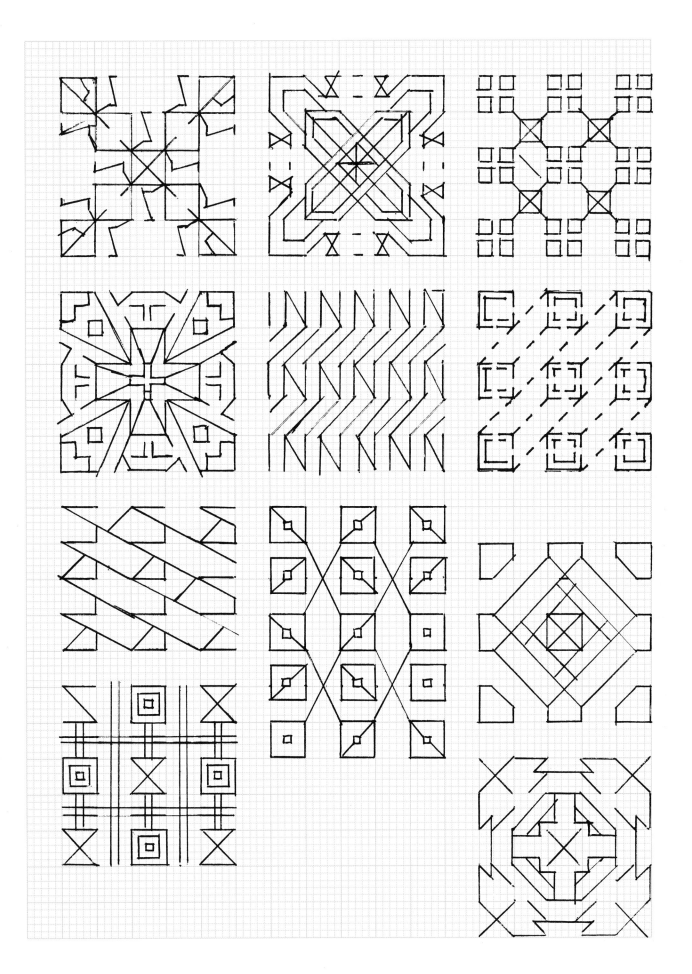

Small projects

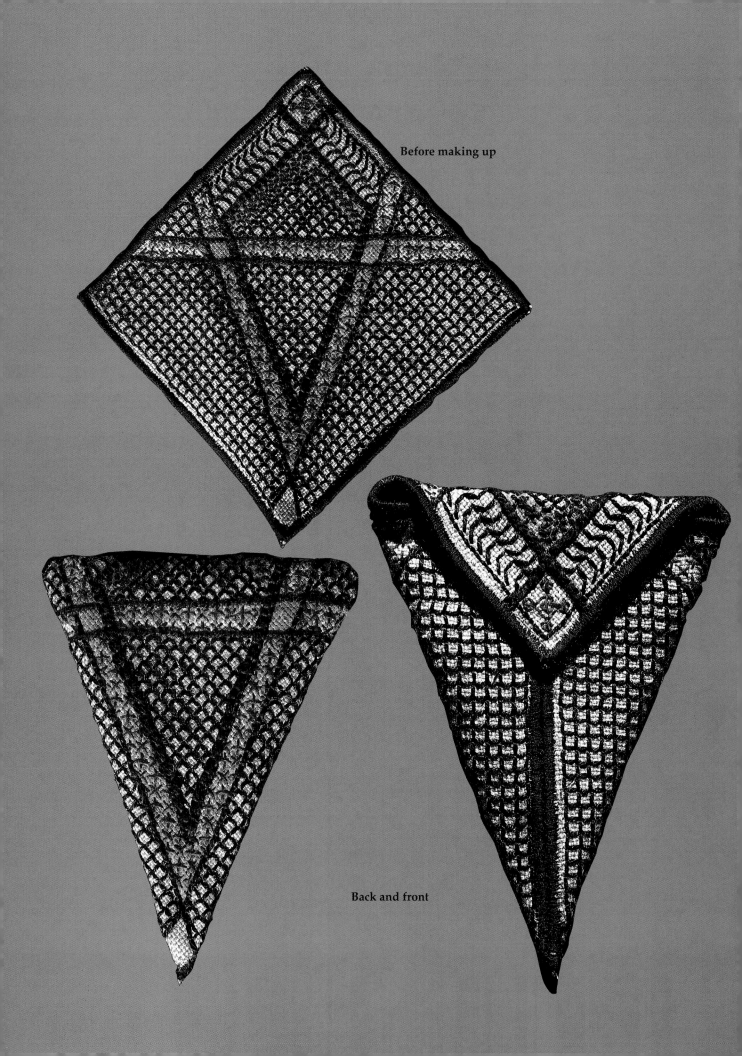

Before making up

Back and front

Blue scissor case

The scissor case is a very simple construction worked on a 13 cm (5″) square of fabric.

Draw the design onto the fabric with Pentel fabric crayons, then iron the colours to fix them on the fabric. Use a piece of paper or thin waste fabric to prevent any spare crayon sticking to the iron.

The stitching is worked with DMC Perle 8 and coton à broder. Machine a lining to the back, satin-stitching a coarse thread to the edge for strength. Fold the square into the envelope shape, following the diagram, and stitch together by hand. Use a press-stud to close the case.

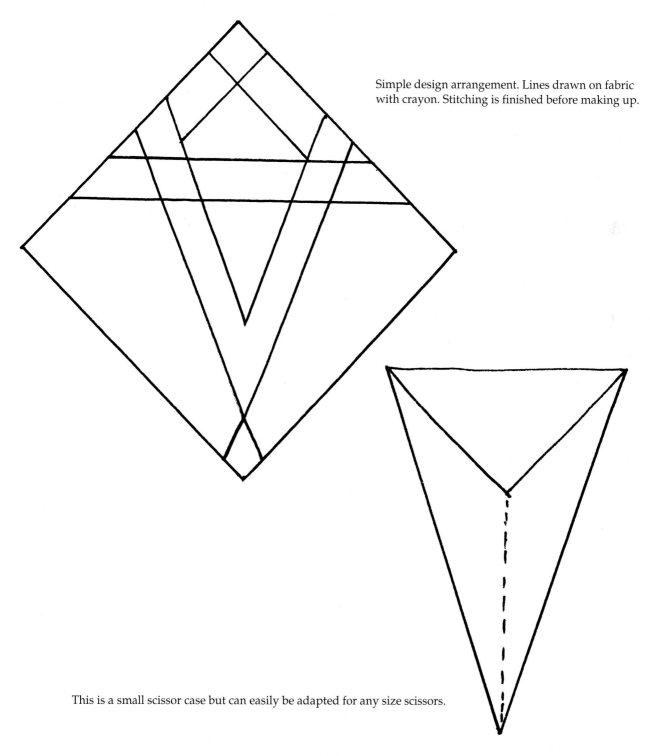

Simple design arrangement. Lines drawn on fabric with crayon. Stitching is finished before making up.

This is a small scissor case but can easily be adapted for any size scissors.

111

Flowers used for brooches on opposite page.

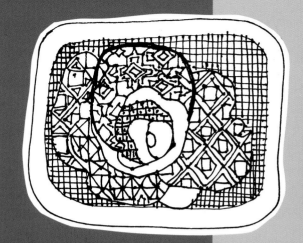

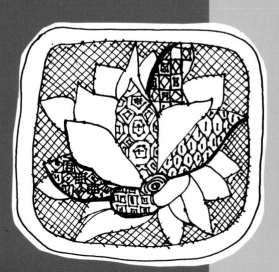

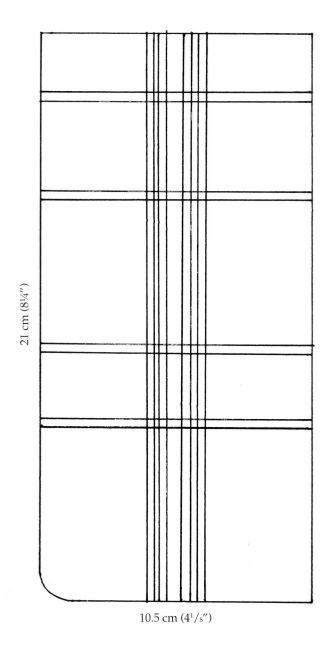

21 cm (8¼")

10.5 cm (4⅛")

Change purse

This could be used as a sampler, adding different stitches to each space. (Or be a use for a sampler!)

Rat-tail, braid stitched down by hand before the patterns were added, defines the stitch areas. The money purse is lined with a linen-textured fabric. The braid is also stitched right along the edge of the purse as a finishing feature and continues as a light handle. Two press studs are used to close the purse.

10.5 cm (4⅛")

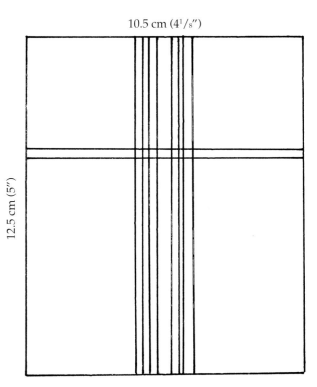

12.5 cm (5")

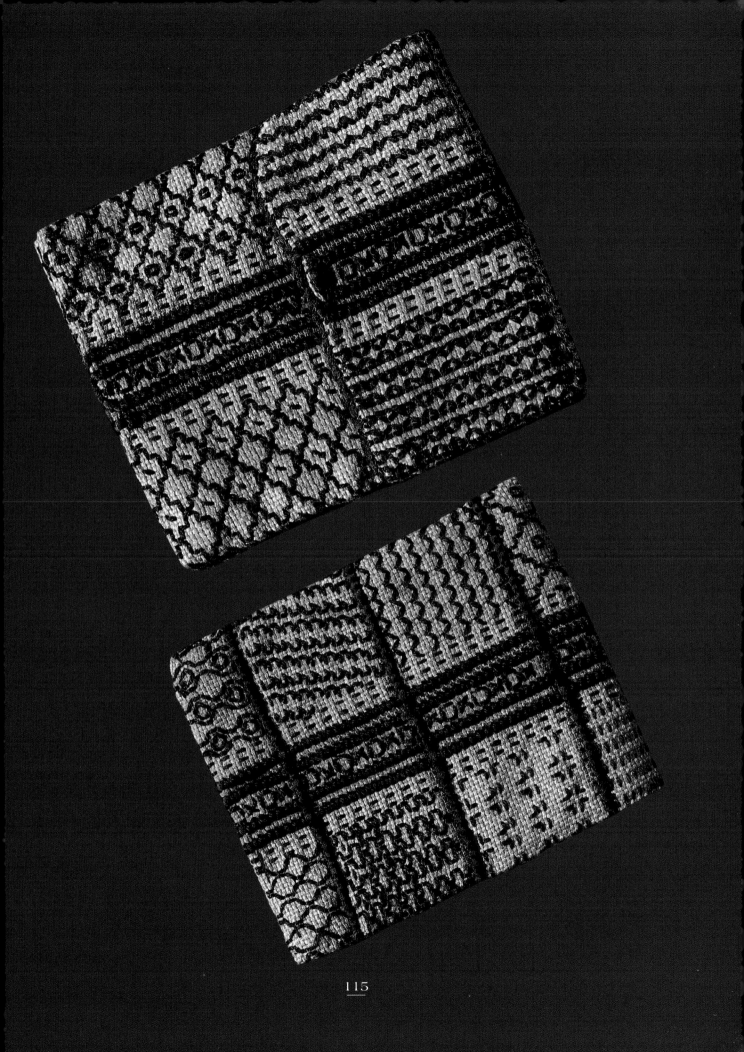

Gum leaf needlecase

Simple gum leaf shapes are used to decorate this needlecase. The leaves are outlined with coral stitch, laced stem stitch and running stitch. Just three tones of one colour were used.

Small triangles of Roumanian stitch suggest the nuts in the background, lying flat on the fabric beneath small raised bundles of thread attached to the surface to suggest the nuts in the foreground.

Two lines of running stitch establish the outline of the embroidery.

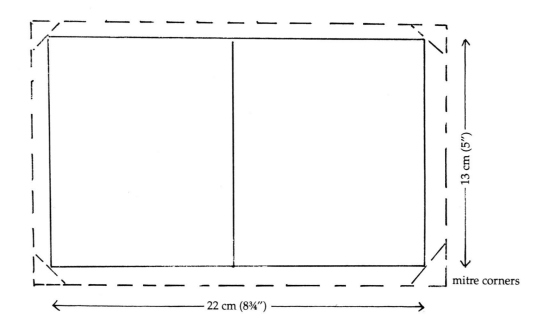

Making up
Mitre the corners and tack the edges down to hem. I used a gaberdine for the lining so no interlining was required.

Cut two pieces of doctor's flannel slightly smaller than the finished case, and machine along the centre line to the lining before stitching it to the needlecase. Slip stitch the lining to the cover, just 5 mm ($^3/_{16}$") inside the edge.

Red needlecase

This needlecase illustrates many examples of pattern darning, using the same format for making up as the gum leaf needlecase on page 116.

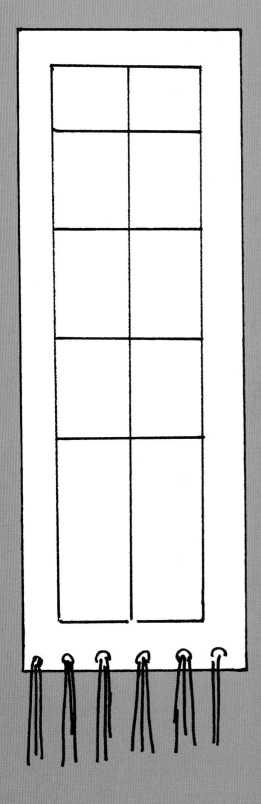

Bookmark

This bookmark with pattern darning and blackwork is another successful way of making a sampler, with a simple fringe to finish the piece. The filling stitches were worked in alternating panels of horizontal and vertical patterns.

The cosmetic collection

The four pieces in this group include a coin purse, key case, lipstick case and a case for sunglasses.

Add 15 mm (³/₈″) all around the patterns for seam allowance.

I used a very simple design, just spreading curved lines across the shapes. Thin acrylic paint in magenta and turquoise was painted across the fabric, with running stitches dividing the spaces. Many different filling stitch patterns in turquoise, green, purple and magenta DMC Perle 8 are used on each piece, adding other tones to the colours with varying densities of stitch. When stitching is complete press on the wrong side of the work.

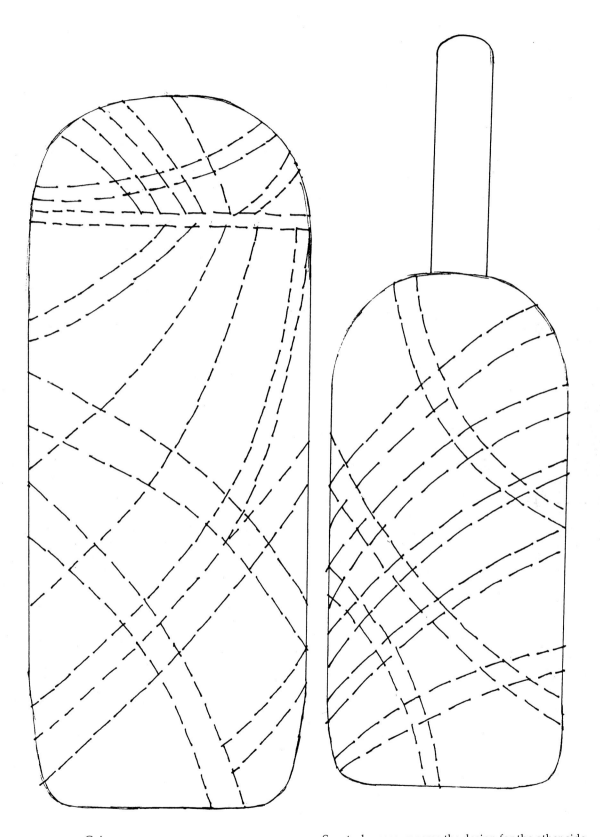

Coin purse   Spectacles case; reverse the design for the other side

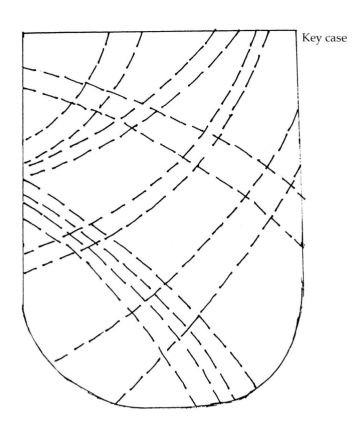

Key case

ENLARGE AT 125%

Gusset for lipstick case

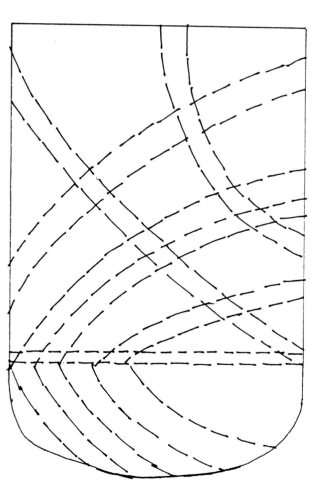

Lipstick case

Making up

Cut pelmet Vilene to the exact size of the patterns. Wrap the embroidery around the Vilene and lace into position. A machined line around the edge of the fabric helps to strengthen the edges when you are pulling the fabric across to lace it.

The coin purse, lipstick case and sunglasses case each have a gusset. The linings, cut from a polyester satin and interlined with iron-on Vilene, were stitched in by hand using slip-hemming.

For the gussets in the coin purse, cut two pieces of lining fabric 8 cm x 7 cm (3″ x 2¾″). Fold and machine, then turn right side out, tuck in the open end and machine again. Stitch these into the sides of the purse by hand. The single gusset for the sunglasses case is 29 cm x 8 cm (11½″ x 3″). Finish with a row of satin stitch at each end before stitching into position. The small gusset in the lipstick case is also made with pelmet Vilene interlining to stiffen it.

The key case has an extra piece of lining fabric 3 cm x 2 cm (1¼″ x ¾″) wrapped around two layers of pelmet Vilene as strengthening to hold the keys. Onto this section stitch two buttons and a strong buttonholed loop to hold the keys.

Finish each piece in the collection with a black press stud.

Blackwork jackets

These sketches show the many possibilities of designing for jackets and collars. When designing for clothing it is important to make the design part of the garment, and not look as though it is an afterthought.

Neckpieces, collars and other suggestions

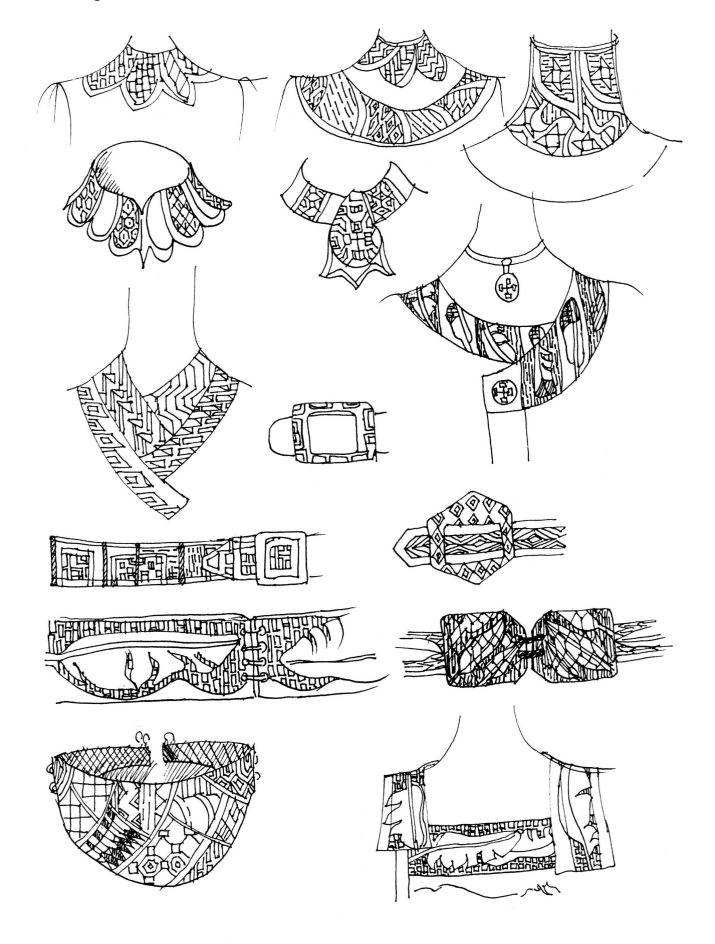

These suggestions for blackwork necklaces all use wrapping as part of the design.

    The outlines and chains are all made by wrapping threads around a cord. The central piece uses a fairly thick cord wrapped with gold thread. Each piece of embroidery is stitched first, then laced over its own piece of cardboard (mountboard is thick enough at this size). As you can see there are endless possibilities in both shape and subject.

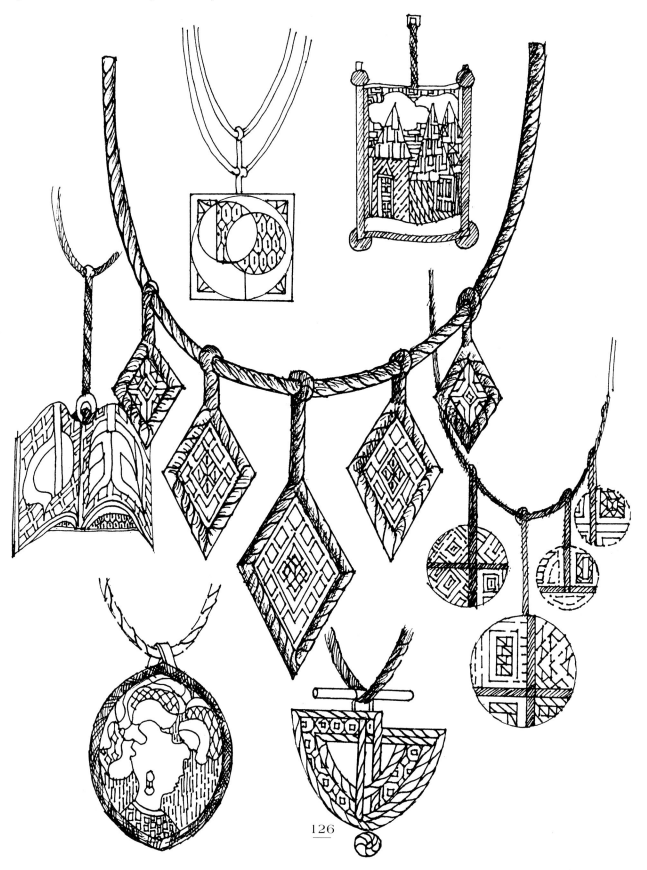

Attaching blackwork motifs to a money belt, backpack, pockets, or on clothing such as braces can be a very useful form of identification for the owner. Other useful items when travelling such as a wristband or bumbag, or a wide watch strap, decorated with the same design, make for simple identification.

127

Index